Also by Tom Jacobs

What's Behind the Numbers?
A Guide to Exposing Financial Chicanery
and Avoiding Huge Losses in Your Portfolio
(with John Del Vecchio)

Rule of 72: How to Compound Your Money
and Uncover Hidden Stock Profits
(with John Del Vecchio)

HOW TO
RETIRE ON
DIVIDENDS:

EARN A SAFE 8%,
LEAVE YOUR
PRINCIPAL INTACT

BRETT OWENS
AND TOM JACOBS

Published by The Marfa Group, Inc.

Book design by Susan Veach
Cover design by Ty Nowicki
Edited by Betsy Goolsby

ISBN: 9781733428408

Printed in the United States of America

Contents

INTRODUCTION

A MILLION DOLLARS is a lot of money. Unfortunately, it won't generate much retirement income today if you limit yourself to popular investments.

The 10-year Treasury is bouncing between 2% and 3%. Put your $1,000,000 in these safe bonds, and you're barely over the poverty level for a family of four, at $28,000 annually (from a 2.8% annual yield). Yikes.

Dividend-paying stocks are masquerading as bond proxies for this reason. But they still don't yield enough. Vanguard's popular Dividend Appreciation ETF (VIG) pays 2.0%, or a mere $20,000 on $1 million. The IShares Select Dividend ETF (DVY) pays 3.4%—better, but that still won't cut it for most people.

When dividends don't generate enough retirement income, you need to sell shares for money to live on. Not good—it means you sell *more* shares of stock when prices are low, and *fewer* when prices are high. That's *reverse* dollar-cost averaging!

Instead of ever selling your stocks, you should *make sure you live on dividends alone so that you never have to touch your capital.*

You can actually live *better* off a (much) more modest nest egg if you know where to look for a lesser-known, meaningful, and secure yield. We're talking about annual income of 6%, 7%, or even 8%—so that you're banking up to $80,000 each year for every $1 million you invest.

This is easier said than done, and obviously the more money you have, the better off you are. But with rates and yields so low, even rich folks have a tough time living off interest today.

While this approach is challenging, it's not impossible. We're going to show you proven strategies for banking *meaningful* high yields in the pages ahead.

This book is for the dividend investor who is too smart to "buy and hope." You (smartly) demand cash *today*—a dividend bird in the hand—from your investments, instead of uncertain capital gains birds in the bush. We're going to show you how to generate enough monthly income with dividends and distributions alone so that you never have to sell another share of stock.

If you want to draw a sustainable income without risking principal and worrying about market ups and downs, this book is for you.

Here we'll show you how to find *great* yields—which we define as 6%, 7%, and even 8% or better—with price upside to boot. We'll walk through where to find investments that are worthy of your retirement portfolio and how to select the best ones. (You don't have to be retired, either. This is great for those who can reinvest dividends for the long term too!)

The book is also for someone who wants to leave a legacy to children, grandchildren, or perhaps a charitable cause. A great benefit of this strategy for those purposes is that your capital remains 100% intact (or better!)

We'll *also* demonstrate that you don't need to follow

the conventional paths—such as "60/40 stocks and bonds" or "4% per year." In fact, you shouldn't. These widely traveled roads are filled with potholes that we'll expose. With a contrarian view, you can have less risk with life-changing results. And yes, there is a way to invest that yields you more (up to four times more, to be specific) than the scant 2.0% the S&P 500 pays you today.

Thanks to a 10-year-old bull market, stocks are pricey. But as long as there are headlines, there will be headline worries. And thanks to them, whether real news or fake, we're able to find pockets of value. Even today.

Throughout the book, we use the phrase "dividend investor" as a shorthand to describe you, our reader. Generally, these are people nearing retirement or already in retirement. That said, we know people way younger who are thrilled to have a portfolio like you'll see here in place, consistently generating a steady 8% per year or more!

Some examples used in the book are taken from past issues of our newsletter service, the *Contrarian Income Report*, and stocks chosen for Huckleberry Capital Management clients. Please treat them as illustrative of the point being made. The actual investment may or may not be one of our buy or hold recommendations today. Please don't rush out and buy these—or any—investments without conducting your own due diligence or seeking further advice!

Rather, we encourage you to do your own investing research to apply the principles we share with you. It's really very simple to turn your stock portfolio into a dividend-paying income machine. Specifically, we're going to show you how to:

Collect great yields and also receive automatic raises every year.

Buy cheap stocks and bonds to give yourself some upside potential to boot.

And enjoy safety and downside protection.

Our Advantage as Nimble Individual Investors

Warren Buffett himself has said that it's easy to invest $1 *million* and net big returns, but with $1 *billion*, one has many fewer opportunities. It's no coincidence that he has $111 billion *in cash* on hand today, burning a hole in his Berkshire Hathaway pocket.

Likewise, the "bond god," Jeffrey Gundlach, manages $120 billion today. CalPERS (California Public Employees Retirement System) has more than $200 billion to deploy. Their size works against them because they have too much money to buy most of the stocks and funds that we individual investors can purchase for the outsized yields we're looking for.

We're talking about investments with market caps around $1 billion, $2 billion, or even $10 billion. They're plenty big for us, but too small for the big guys to buy. If they started to accumulate shares, they'd move the entire market and quickly eliminate any value!

Fortunately, you and we don't manage billions—so we don't have this problem. We're free and clear to buy the shares that Buffett, Gundlach, and CalPERS would if they could. But they can't!

Our freedom lets us pursue a 100% dividend-funded retirement. This helps us avoid the most common retirement investing pitfall—risking too much capital for not enough income.

CHAPTER 1

The Problem: Not Enough Low-Risk (Dividend-Powered) Income

WE RETIREES AND soon-to-be retirees have a dilemma. The traditional pension is just about gone. Social Security won't support the lifestyle most of us want. We are left to our own devices.

But even if we do build up a fat balance in a 401(k) or other retirement plan, how do we make it last? Especially when, as one client put it, "the bank pays zero point nothing." Today, you can't find anything that pays significant "interest."

> **Retirees need income *now*.**

This is becoming a crisis in the US. We are told that stocks provide the best returns over the long term, but retirees need income *now*. Most retirement investors prefer dividend income to long-term gains, but yields haven't been this low in decades! The S&P 500 pays a measly 2.0% today. If you have a million-dollar portfolio, that's a lousy $20,000 per year in income, or $385 a week. That's no retirement.

Keep in mind that most investors are invested in the

S&P 500, whether in an index fund or individual stocks, because they own the very biggest stocks that dominate the S&P 500's moves. You can do better—*four times better*, to be specific—*and* raise your dividend income by 400% simply by selling these mainstream (translation: "mediocre") plays and buying *bigger payouts that are better values.*

Specifically, we're going to discuss stocks, bonds, and funds that pay a safe 6%, 7%, and 8%, instead of the broader market's 2%. That's up to $80,000 in passive income on a million bucks, and $40,000 annually on $500,000 (versus $20,000 and $10,000 per year—an easy choice).

But first, let us show you the logical—but wrong—assumption that most mainstream dividend investors make.

Dividend "Aristocrats" Aren't

Most dividend-income investors may protest, "But I don't own the S&P 500 index for income. I choose the best companies in the index, the ones whose dividends have gone up and up. The dividend aristocrats." Let's look at some of the dividend royalty to see whether they are true monarchs or mere pretenders to the throne.

> A dividend aristocrat is a company that has continuously increased the size of dividends it pays to its shareholders. To be considered a dividend aristocrat, a company must typically raise dividends consistently for at least 25 years. *www.investopedia.com*

Take a consumer staple like General Mills (GIS). It pays a "generous" 4.5%, and look at this lovely staircase dividend chart.

A Cheerios-Powered Dividend Staircase

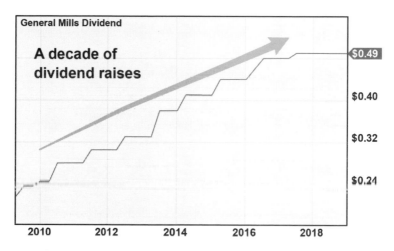

This compelling chart is what gives companies their reputations as dividend kings. You can count on their dividends so much that they become "must have" stocks, revered royalty.

The catch: the dividend-only chart isn't for sale! You don't just buy the dividend. You also buy the price.

So, those investors who looked only at the dividend bought the wrong chart for investment income. They wanted the stock's *payout*, but were steamrolled by the stock's 49% *price* decline while they waited. Why?

Remember, *you are never buying the dividend only.* With a stock like General Mills, you are *buying a business,* and stock price is all about business performance. And real-world businesses rarely prosper long enough to become a dividend aristocrat without a manic stock chart.

General Mills' sluggish business performance means it isn't really a "must have" stock any more. Sagging demand for Cheerios and Green Giant Peas has weighed on profit— and dividend—growth in recent years. As they've slowed down, so has the stock price, a cliff-fall 49% in just over two years.

A Decade of Dividends Gets Crunched

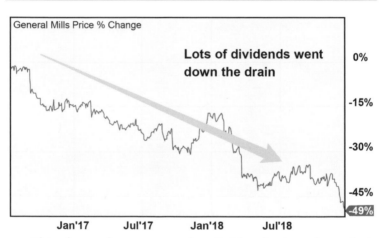

This shows that even regular dividend raisers have their issues too.

Now let's take Johnson & Johnson (JNJ), which has nearly doubled its dividend over the last 10 years (+96%). Shares pay 2.8% as we write, but they lost 7.6% in 2018 in price when a judge awarded $4.7 billion to plaintiffs, connecting a bad batch of baby powder to cancer.

Legal Decision Sent JNJ Lower in 2018

To buy the dividend staircase, you end up buying the manic price chart. (You never get something for nothing.) And sure, there were great times to buy Johnson & Johnson for profits, such as when the market ripped off its Band-Aid in the 2008–09 crash and the stock paid 3.8%. But can we really sit in cash and wait for the next financial crisis to present us with a buying moment? No one gets the timing right on both going to cash and "getting back in."

For most of the last five years, Johnson & Johnson has paid between 2.25% and 3%. Unless you're rich—$3 million invested in the Band-Aid king would bring in $67,500 to $90,000—this investment doesn't generate enough income to fund a comfortable retirement. A 3% yield only generates $30,000 in dividend income on a million-dollar position. And even if you *are* rich—congrats!—why should you accept such paltry returns?

Don't Look Here for a 4% Yield

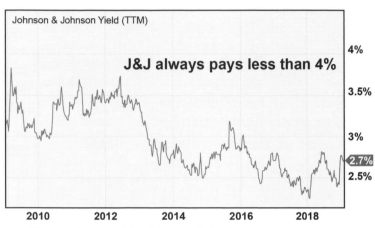

Johnson & Johnson Yield (TTM)

J&J always pays less than 4%

4%

3.5%

3%

2.7%

2.5%

2010   2012   2014   2016   2018

The problem with this stock is that, controversy or not, it's *always* expensive on a valuation basis, whether using earnings per share, free cash flow, or other metrics. The downside stock risk from valuation alone is greater than the benefit of the dividend. Which means you're exposing yourself to short-term price risk to collect a measly 2.8% dividend.

Baby powder problems aside, by buying Johnson & Johnson, you're putting your retirement portfolio in the way of a potential stock market crash. A bear market will take down that company and everything else with it. And in the conventional wisdom of annual 4% withdrawals— where you're told to withdraw principal too—you're selling *more* shares at exactly the *wrong* time (when the price is low!). We'll discuss the dangers of this "reverse dollar-cost averaging" in a moment.

Bottom line, if you're after dividends, this purchase isn't worth the risk for a stingy 2.8%. Even if you buy $1 million in shares in the baby shampoo goddess, you're only collecting $28,000 in annual income. That's simply too much of a pay cut.

The problem with investing in dividend aristocrats like these is that they're already considered the highest-quality companies in the world—which means that their stocks are popular and therefore almost always expensive, and their current yields are typically quite modest.

Tempted to hang about waiting for these dividend aristocrats' stocks to go on sale? They rarely do, and waiting can be hazardous to your health. You are paying the "opportunity cost," which is what you could have earned by investing it better elsewhere.

(Remember, Johnson & Johnson hasn't been on sale in 10 years—and even in the depths of the financial crisis, the stock *still* didn't pay 4%. You will see that *we* only look for yields of 5% to 10%.)

Well, you might say, "You just have to choose the right aristocrats. There are others besides General Mills and Johnson & Johnson." Unfortunately, it's not a matter of dividend aristocrat–picking prowess either. They are all usually overpriced, a function of their popularity and automatic inclusion in stock market indexes.

Let's take four more blue-chip "dividend aristocrats": Coca-Cola (KO), Kimberly-Clark (KMB), McDonald's (MCD), and Walmart (WMT). To say their best growth days are behind them would be kind. Check out their flat-to-declining sales trends. It is difficult to declare a dividend "safe" when the business behind the payout is struggling.

Sales Challenges for This Royal Bunch

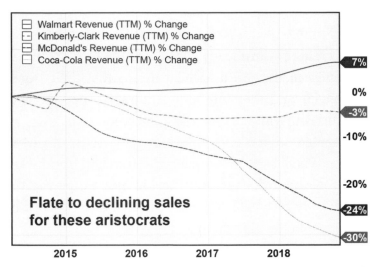

Walmart Revenue (TTM) % Change
Kimberly-Clark Revenue (TTM) % Change
McDonald's Revenue (TTM) % Change
Coca-Cola Revenue (TTM) % Change

7%

0%

-3%

-10%

-20%

**Flate to declining sales
for these aristocrats**

-24%

-30%

2015   2016   2017   2018

But you'd never guess these firms were having sales struggles by looking at their valuations. They are still popular and pricey. Let's consider their price-to-earnings (P/E) ratios, which look quite rich, considering these uncertain growth prospects.

COMPANY	CURRENT YIELD	5-YEAR SALES GROWTH	P/E RATIO
Coca-Cola	3.4%	-30%	71
Kimberly-Clark	3.4%	-3%	30
McDonald's	2.5%	-24%	25
Walmart	2.2%	7%	43

These lofty P/E ratios not only reflect investor convictions in growth (though the companies offer little) but also misplaced belief in safety (yes, they'll likely be around come what may, but not at these high prices). Is this kind of risk worth a four-stock aristocrat portfolio that only pays an average 2.8%? *We think not.*

And this is *after* considering dividend growth. Over the past decade, these four companies have boosted their payout ratios (the percentage of earnings they pay as dividends) to support their aristocrat status. Sure, their dividends are growing, but they can't do it forever by increasing the amount of extra cash they pay out (that's the payout ratio). You can only pay 100%, and we don't want to see a company get even halfway to that. All four are well over our "half profits, half payouts" threshold today.

COMPANY	PAYOUT RATIO
Coca-Cola	230%
Kimberly-Clark	85%
McDonald's	61%
Walmart	118%

Look at what this means. Your $1 million portfolio will only earn you $28,000 in dividend income annually invested in these shares, but you think, "If I hold long enough, that 2.8% on my original investment will grow." But the dividend growth is iffy.

These companies' best days are behind them. If they weren't, the payout ratios would stand still or even decline, while the dividends grow. That's not the case for our four companies. Anytime we see more than a 50% payout ratio, we're wary that a company might have to cut the dividend in a downturn. And then, "look out below" for the stock price!

Let us repeat. A $1 million portfolio at 2.8% will earn you only $28,000 in dividend income annually invested in these shares. That's only $538 a week in retirement. And it's not even that secure.

There's another problem with stocks like these: they go up *and* down. These price gyrations worked in your favor as you were building your portfolio—you were able to buy more shares for your investment dollar when stock prices were cheap. Unfortunately, this tailwind becomes a headwind if you try to sell shares to fund your retirement. Here's why.

The "4% Withdrawal" Fallacy

The solution that mainstream financial advisors pitch is a "4% withdrawal rate," based on research performed by William Bengen, an aeronautical engineer who graduated from MIT (bright guy!). He ran a family business and then decided to earn a Master's in financial planning and become a financial planner to help people. His clients asked him regularly what they could withdraw from their accounts to have "enough" money to live on in retirement.

Bengen found that a 50-50 mix of stocks and bonds and a 4% annual withdrawal rate worked. In no case from 1926 to 1976—with inflation, deflation, higher or lower prevailing interest and dividend rates, and booms and busts—did a 4% withdrawal rate exhaust a portfolio in under 33 years.* This has been often been called "The Bengen Rule," the maximum safe withdrawal rate, and the "SWR" for safe withdrawal rate, and it's been validated by further research such as the Trinity Study. However, new research led him to modify his rule to a 4.5% withdrawal in the first year and then to increase the dollar amount by inflation annually. Most planners and advisors haven't caught up and stick to the 4% maxim.

It's important to have a rule that can apply across the board. If you're a planner or advisor, you want your client to have peace of mind. And if you are a Wells Fargo or Merrill Lynch, you need to apply the practice across thousands of clients and over a trillion dollars in accounts. So, you pick the most conservative method. Your client can be safe and you can be safe from liability.

Advisors are human beings and humans follow the path of least resistance. So, rather than dust off Bengen's formula and model a custom spreadsheet for every client, the advisor will simply "toggle" the risk meter up or down by ticking the yearly withdrawal rate up or down.

Want to be a bit more conservative? Stick with 3.5% per year. Feeling bullish? Go with 4% or 4.5%. But this advice is overly simplistic. You can have excellent retirement income *and* portfolio longevity without complex research and assumptions.

Retirement isn't rocket science, especially if you know what stocks and bonds to buy. Since you're reading this,

---

* His 1994 paper was called "Determining withdrawal rates using historical data," www.retailinvestor.org/pdf/Bengen1.pdf. An interview with Bengen about the change to the 4% rule appears at https://earlyretirementdude.com/summary-tuesdays-reddit-interview-inventor-4-rule/

you're probably looking for a withdrawal rate *above* 4%. This is quite doable and you don't have to accept $40,000 a year. With 8% annual income, most people can live comfortably and not withdraw any principal. That's why we call it the "8% No Withdrawal Portfolio." Withdraw the income, not your hard-earned savings. Your account lasts far longer and provides more income than the 4% rule could dream of! (For more, see Appendix A.)

The 4% rule *does* require the withdrawal of principal. During bull markets this is generally fine, but every now and then the market does not always play along with our carefully laid retirement plans and you're faced with a chart that looks like this:

Microsoft's Price Diverged from Its Dividend

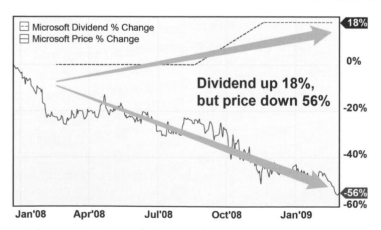

This was Microsoft during the 2008 stock market crash. The company's dividend was just fine—in fact, the firm hiked it by a generous 18% amidst the broader chaos. But the high-quality stock attached to it was thrown out with the bearish bathwater as *shares lost 56% from peak to trough.*

But what about shareholders in retirement who were following the 4% fallacy? They were forced to sell *more* shares to make up their income shortfall *at exactly the wrong time.*

Remember the benefits of dollar-cost averaging that built your retirement portfolio? (See Appendix A for a reminder.) You bought stock regularly over many years, mostly through contributions to your company's 401(k) plan. Doing so smoothed out your purchase prices, so you didn't get caught investing only at high times, and you kept investing at low times (very important). Using the 4% withdrawal rule with low-yield investments, this wise principle shifts into reverse! The same phenomenon that built your wealth now works against you. You're forced to sell even more shares when prices are low, reducing your upside when markets normalize.

It's a recipe for running out of money, and along the way, there is a drip, drip, drip of financial "blood" too. Remember the annual $40,000 you thought you were banking on your million? As you deplete your million through withdrawals, there is less money to earn dividends for you. The $40,000 slowly declines.

And, oh, by the way, your spending in retirement probably won't be the same from year to year. The *New York Times* recently reported on the "myth of steady retirement spending" and learned that you may need more money early on. More spending up front means more withdrawals will be needed sooner, and you'll have less capital to compound later.

The solution to get away from having to rely on an upward-trending stock market? Transition away from ever having to sell a share! Meaningful dividends of 8% or better are the way to pullback-proof your portfolio. They give you a means to "cash out" your nest egg on a monthly and quarterly basis, without being forced to sell the egg low (or sell ever).

And if you *don't* need to withdraw all your income, it's possible to take advantage of "right way" dollar-cost averaging and reinvest part of the dividend income, which would have been very sweet indeed during Microsoft's collapse.

We invite you to step beyond Wall Street's low-yielding "blue-chip BS" and create a portfolio that can generate *meaningful* income. Ditch the aristocrats that pay you like you're running a lemonade stand for a living and secure yourself a four-times pay raise while still keeping your capital intact to boot.

In the chapters that follow, we'll show you how to find the right stocks to construct a **secure 8% retirement portfolio** using future dividend aristocrats and sidestep the danger of a low-yield world where you have no choice but to withdraw 4% (or more if you want to live better) of your capital every year. That's why we call this approach the "No Withdrawal" portfolio.

Let's get started …

CHAPTER 2

The Solution: 8% "No Withdrawal" Retirement Portfolio

IT'S NOT YOUR fault that the US Federal Reserve bank has crushed savers by lowering interest rates to the basement to stimulate the economy after the Great Recession. If you were preparing for retirement in any normal era, you'd have some legitimate options in fixed income. Today? Not so much. It looked for a year or so that rates would rise, perhaps providing more lower risk income, but now they are slated to languish or decline.

Plus, if you're worried about a stock market pullback or crash—and we don't blame you, with equities near record-high valuations—then we need to transition your portfolio away from the casino of stock prices into the steady staircase of dividends. That transition is into a world where rising or falling rates or markets just don't matter much.

The proper solution is one you've probably thought of: a No Withdrawal portfolio that relies entirely on dividend income and leaves your principal 100% intact.

"I'm in!" you say. "Dividend income sounds great," you're no doubt thinking. "But don't stocks only pay sexy high yields like these at the depths of bear markets—or when they are in so much trouble that their stock prices are low for a reason?" That's partially true—blue chips tend to only pay yields of 4% or better near stock market bottoms, and high yields should never be accepted without scrutiny.

But while many of you may be skeptical of the idea of 8% "interest," it exists, and why most people don't make use of it is really very simple (as we'll show you). This kind of income exists and is not any riskier—in fact, these firms are *less* likely to cut their dividends or see stock price declines—than the dividend aristocrats.

There are three main stock market vehicles available today that pay reliable yields of 8% or higher. We'll discuss them in detail in the chapters ahead. First, let's get used to one important income investing concept that is so obvious we rarely hear about it.

Let's take the big firms that manage most individual investment money in the US today. Think Wells Fargo, Morgan Stanley, Merrill Lynch, and also your neighborhood Edward Jones, Raymond James, and even Fidelity, Schwab, and Vanguard—and yes, the new roboadvisors such as Betterment and Wealth Front. These outfits may customize investments for you if you have a gazillion dollars, but for everyone else, it's cookie-cutter. They plug your age, money, future earnings, and expenses into fancy software that spits out a nice-looking profile, with colored pie charts and everything. Plus, they have these nice offices. They must know what they are doing, right?

They do, to a point. But they are serving hundreds of thousands of clients, with millions and millions of dollars, around the country and the world. So, if they are offering the same approaches for people of similar situations, they can only offer investments for which there are "enough of" for everyone!

This is "liquidity." A stock like Apple is so liquid that you can buy or sell any amount you want, anytime. There are always enough buyers and sellers putting orders in to match yours. You can turn your Apple stock into cash in an instant.

On the other hand, your house is not liquid. It might sell tomorrow, next year, or who knows when, and at what price. And that's true of some stocks that are less liquid. There is simply less of some companies' shares to go around.

That means one simple thing. The familiar names can't recommend our high-income producers to you. Instead, they stick you in pretty much what everyone has. And one more thing. If these are stocks, owning them is not much different than owning a low-cost index fund from Vanguard. The same stocks dominate the same market indexes Vanguard uses! If you own a handful of the big names today, such as Apple, Amazon, Facebook, Berkshire Hathaway, and Microsoft, well, you basically own the S&P 500, because these companies' stock movements determine in large part the direction of the S&P 500. As goes Apple, so goes the S&P.

Most people prefer to own all the familiar names, and not for wrong reasons. They think, "Well, they are so big, and I am familiar with their products, so I don't have to worry about them blowing up and taking my money with them." They think that smaller investments are riskier. This isn't wrong. But it plays into this thinking: "Something is big and popular, so it's good." Or is it good just because it's popular?

Apple has a market value of more than $700 billion. And shares yield just 1.9%. Convenience, familiarity, and liquidity come at the expense of the stock's current payout.

Let's contrast Apple with hospital landlord Medical Properties Trust (MPW). The firm pays a generous 5.9% on capital you invest today—three times as much as Apple! And its focus, the hospital, is arguably even more indispensable than the iPhone (which does have competition from Samsung and others).

But Medical Properties the *stock* isn't large enough for the big pension funds to buy or for the brand-name money managers to pile into. With a modest market cap of $6 billion, Medical Properties is *plenty* liquid for you and me— and exclusive enough to provide us with this generous yield premium!

Plus, just like Apple, it raises its dividend every year. In fact, *Contrarian Income Report** readers who bought the stock when we recommended it are now enjoying a 9.0% yield on cost (what they paid originally).

---

*   Brett publishes a free daily newsletter with actionable dividend ideas. Visit ContrarianOutlook.com to grab your complimentary subscription.

Yield on Cost

9.0%

Bought Nov 6, 2015

**MPW
Current Yield:**

5.9%

New investors who are patient will likely be able to buy Medical Properties on a pullback in the future and bank more dividend for their dollar. The stock's 5.9% current yield, while generous by blue-chip standards, is actually on the low end of its historical range.

Under-the-Radar MPW Pays Generously

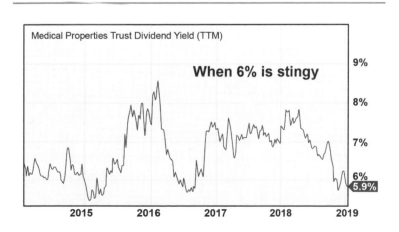

Medical Properties Trust Dividend Yield (TTM)

With a generous dividend and annual raises, is it any wonder that this stock also trounced the broader market? Not only are we enjoying a 9% yield today on our initial purchase price, but Medical Properties has also treated us to 93% total returns (including dividends) since we bought it (versus 35% for the S&P 500 over the same time period).

93% Total Returns From Medical Properties

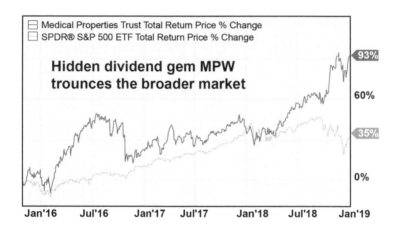

Our nimble size is our edge as individual investors. We smartly focus on investment vehicles that have market caps between $1 billion and $10 billion. (We can buy these; the big fish can't.) Many of these stocks and funds pay 6%, 7%, and even 8% current yields. Their obscurity is our big advantage.

A "billion" is pretty huge for you and me, but it's not something that Wells Fargo advisors can invest their clients around the country in. Big-time money managers like Buffett and Jeffrey Gundlach can't buy them, either. They'd move the market, which is why they must focus on mainstream names like Apple. Their cash constraints create opportunity for us.

These "under the radar" dividend vehicles are plenty liquid enough for you and me—they can handle our buying and selling just fine—but not for the big institutional investors that hold two-thirds of all shares in public stocks. And the financial media really only care about what's well known and most liquid. So, smaller companies (yes, a few billion in market value is small, relatively) make up only a fraction of the stock market's total capitalization and don't get much coverage from the financial media. There's more of a chance for us to find something juicy in an orchard that hasn't been picked over. And there is plenty of high-yield fruit once we aren't looking where everyone else is.

While these ignored corners of the financial markets are ideal places for us to search for high yields, they are like any other sectors. There are good investment candidates and bad ones too.

So, let's talk about these areas—and how to employ a contrarian approach to finding the best values: the secure, meaningful yields up to 8% with price stability and even 10% to 15% upside in many cases.

A $1 Million

"No Withdrawal"

Portfolio

$1,000,000
in capital
▶
$80,000
in yearly income

+

Our original $1,000,000
stays intact (or better)

Of course, not all high-yield investments are buys. Some vehicles are nothing more than dividend traps, paying high stated yields that are simply not sustainable. We'll call out these "paper payout tigers" later in this book (Chapter 6) and teach you how to avoid them.

Once you know how to navigate the dividend space, you can earn the types of returns that you have been told are not possible (like the Wright Brothers were told they would never fly) and safely collect big yields—which means you may never have to tap into your retirement capital to pay your bills.

First up, we need to dispel some other common retirement investment myths standing between you and a comfortable, dividend-powered retirement.

CHAPTER 3

Our Edge: Second-Level Thinking

EVERYBODY'S GOT A "system" they want to sell you. What the 8% No Withdrawal Retirement Portfolio offers is hidden in plain sight. Let's start with the edge we want you to have.

Renowned value investor Howard Marks, chief of Oaktree Capital Group, with $120 billion under management, boasts over four decades in the investment trenches. His brilliance earned him a regular spot on the *Forbes* World's Billionaires list several years running.

The sometimes folksy, yet always prescient, commentary in his *Oaktree Memos* is read religiously by some of the greatest investors of our time. *Business Insider* once described these memos saying, "[T]he letters read like Michael Lewis ghostwriting for Warren Buffett."

For dividend investors like us, the most important insight from Marks is hidden in a chapter of his excellent book *The Most Important Thing: Uncommon Sense for the Thoughtful Investor*. It's a work that won acclaim from legendary value investors Joel Greenblatt, Jeremy Grantham, Seth Klarman, and even Warren Buffett.

In the book, Marks identifies the typical value investor's first-level thinking: if you analyze a stock and it looks cheap, you should buy it.

But everyone is doing this, in one form or another. Growth, value, dividends—all investors look at the same data. Marks introduces what he calls "second-level thinking," with a few examples:

- First-level thinking says, *"It's a good company; let's buy the stock."* Second-level thinking says, *"It's a good company, but everyone thinks it's a great company, and it's not. So the stock's overrated and overpriced; let's sell."*

- First-level thinking says, *"The outlook calls for low growth and rising inflation. Let's dump our stocks."* Second-level thinking says, *"The outlook stinks, but everyone else is selling in panic. Buy!"*

- First-level thinking says, *"I think the company's earnings will fall; sell."* Second-level thinking says, *"I think the company's earnings will fall less than people expect, and the pleasant surprise will lift the stock; buy."* (Marks, pgs. 3–4)

Marks's second-level mindset has helped Oaktree make a number of gutsy, profitable moves—like the $10.9 billion distressed debt fund it raised in 2008, the largest to date. In fact, Oaktree has earned its clients an astounding 19% annualized *after fees* on its distressed debt funds, and Howard Marks has made himself a billionaire twice over using this approach.

A track record like his makes it almost tempting to just sign over your portfolio and let Oaktree Capital take care of the rest, no? Alas, Oaktree provides its services to institutional and (very, very) high-net-worth clients only.

But you and we can tap Marks's mindset to earn more yield than first-level dividend seekers. After all, most income hounds look for yield, find a stock paying above average (say 4%), and immediately conclude that they should buy it.

Other investors practice "buy and hope" investing. They pick up shares and root for them to appreciate in price. And that's it. These first-level types—they stay above the surface—have no plan for how to generate cash flow from their holdings. They think they'll sell someday and "hope" it's at a higher price. But they don't have a game plan to sell and methodically harvest cash from the portfolio they worked so hard to build. Even if there were a smart plan for the 4% withdrawal method, most people have no idea what to sell.

This is where we want to be better thinkers. Throughout the book, we refer to first-level thinking or first-level investors and also to second-level. This is simply our shorthand to refer to either a superficial way of thinking about investments and investment advice —"level 1 thinking"— or a rather more considered way of thinking through an investment choice, which is "level 2 thinking."

Take the rule of thumb that says as you get older and move towards retirement, your portfolio should be made up of bonds (fixed income) and stocks, with the percentage of bonds you hold equal to your age and the rest in stocks.

As an example, if you are 60 years old (congratulations, by the way), then your portfolio should contain 60% in bonds and 40% in stocks. By the time you hit 70, your portfolio should have migrated to 70% in bonds and 30% stocks and so on.

We refer to this kind of thinking as first-level thinking. Second-level thinking will tell you that this does not properly account for your personal set of circumstances, let alone the very real effect of our increasing lifespans and inflation. First level is the surface of the water. Second level is the well-known but less-practiced "deep dive."

You need to have investments in the right kinds of companies, where, as dividends increase, stock prices naturally follow. This provides the required growth to counter inflation and avoid some serious problems if you end up living longer than expected.

We've already discussed the 4% rule of thumb that says provided you withdraw no more than 4% per annum you shouldn't run out of money. Again, this is first-level thinking.

You already know what we believe. Second-level thinking tells us that the 4% rule is probably for financial service companies dealing with thousands of clients. They have to deliver the same thing to everyone, not least because they need to have policies in place to satisfy their research and legal departments. It's simply too risky to take any action that doesn't fit their generic approach. Don't blame them. There isn't any other way for a Wells Fargo to do business (though they could improve in other ways we've learned about!).

Instead, what we care about is maximizing the future dividends we're going to receive in exchange for each new stock purchase and each new dividend reinvestment. We do this by combing the contrarian corners of the income-investing world so that we can deploy our capital to get the best deals. We pay the least we can today in exchange for the most in future payouts. And we don't want to take undue risks either. Simply, our sole goal is to acquire as many shares in secure higher-income-paying assets as we can. Why wouldn't we?

We don't really care where stock (or fund) prices go in the short term. They are *irrelevant* to our income streams, which are protected because we spend our time forecasting cash flows and investor payouts, rather than daily price ticks.

Of course, we don't recommend chasing all decent income payers. We know that not every unloved asset is a good deal. For example, while companies like Exxon, Chevron, and BP have been able to pay their dividends over the recent past, their stocks have often been crushed. Investors saw these so-called "stalwart" businesses crumble as the black goo (not always gold) slid below $30 per barrel. Oil and gas will rise and fall. So will these companies' stocks, and likely at just the time you need to sell your shares.

On the other hand, at times there are big dividend payers who are undeservedly swept aside. Their underlying businesses (or portfolios) are fine, and they continue to pay their regular dividends like clockwork. These are the payout streams we want to buy.

Historically, dividends have accounted for about half of the stock market's long-term returns,* so it makes sense that we'll outperform the S&P with a higher-yielding portfolio. And by buying issues when they're out of favor, we maximize our upside to boot.

---

* https://www.hartfordfunds.com/dam/en/docs/pub/whitepapers/WP106.pdf

It's fun watching your portfolio climb in value on paper but frustrating if you're looking for a bargain to buy in real life. People putting money into the stock market over time want to pay as low a valuation as possible. *These "net buyers" of stocks want depressed prices.* (If there's one rule we'd want every investor to learn, it's that one!)*

This is all well and good, but how can we collect meaningful income and profit from America's increasingly responsible and flush homeowners?

We'll get there, but that's a tease. First, let's start in one of our favorite and often neglected corners of the financial market: bonds, but not in the way you are probably used to thinking about them.

> Net buyers of stocks want lower prices.

---

* A **net buyer of stocks** is an investor who is buying more stock in the account than withdrawing from it. This can be through adding new money and reinvesting dividends. This buyer is typically building account value for retirement and wants to pay the lowest price (valuation) for shares. A **net seller** is someone who is withdrawing more from the account than new money added or dividends received. The seller is typically retired, uses the account for living expenses, and wants to sell at the highest price (valuation).

CHAPTER 4

A Better Way to Buy Bonds: Closed-End Funds

A SMART BOND portfolio will take the stress out of retirement investing. It's like an annuity, but better. We receive regular monthly payments *plus* we get to keep our original capital.

But as with stocks, we also have a lack of yield in bonds today. After a furious "rally," the US 10-year Treasury bond only pays 2.8%. This is a mere $28,000 in interest payments on a million dollars, which is simply not enough income for most retirees.

Fortunately, it is actually easy for us to double up "regular" bond returns *by swapping out popularity for quality*. Most investors, looking for simple ways to build a diversified bond portfolio, focus their attention on popular options such as mutual funds and exchange-traded funds (ETFs),* promoted heavily by marketing powerhouses such as Vanguard, Fidelity, and iShares.

---

* **Mutual funds and exchange-traded funds (ETFs)** are both pools of money which is then invested in other assets. The original idea was for the individual investor to be able to own a broad mix of different assets. Mutual funds trade once a day after market close. An exchange-traded fund (ETF) is a mutual fund that trades like a stock, so you may buy and sell shares when the market is open. Each has advantages and disadvantages versus the other.

But most of these funds do not meet our two strict requirements for inclusion in our No Withdrawal Portfolio. First, as with Treasuries, they simply don't pay enough. We need yields of 6%, 7%, and even 8% or better to generate enough income.

Second, these funds—as a function of their popularity—all trade for fair value. That's a problem for contrarians like us looking for a bargain! Ideally, we'd like to see our bond funds yield 6% or better and have the potential for 10% or more when you add *upside price appreciation too.*

This eliminates most mutual funds and ETFs. We'll leave those pedestrian vehicles to the first-level types. We second-level thinkers prefer closed-end funds, or CEFs.

What are CEFs and how do they work?

If you are unfamiliar with closed-end funds, or CEFs, you can think of them as being like an open-end fund—a mutual fund or an ETF—with some important differences.

Similar to its cousin vehicles, a CEF is a pooled investment fund with a manager overseeing the portfolio. Its shares trade on the open market, but unlike a mutual fund, which can issue new shares as it grows in popularity, CEF managers do not create new shares to meet demand from investors (though new shares may be issued to raise new money to invest, but that's a choice, not a requirement).

Rather, closed-end fund investors must sell their shares to someone else, much like a stock. So CEF managers don't have to worry about a capital crunch and being forced to sell perfectly good positions for cheap to cash out fleeing shareholders, like their mutual fund or ETF manager counterparts must. CEF managers have a set pool of money, thanks to the public markets, and they can sit tight on their positions through any panic.

It does of course mean that CEF prices are subject to market whims. This also means that like stocks, they can trade at premiums or discounts to the value of their assets (called net asset value, or NAV), depending on the market's mood.

> Net asset value (NAV) is the total price a fund's investments would fetch if they were liquidated today, minus any debt. It's the same as your own personal net worth, which is what would be left over if you sold everything you owned and paid off your debts.

As you know, professional and individual investors are often manic. They hate a stock one minute and love it the next. As their emotions swing, they may bid up the prices of our stocks. As they do, the percentage yield on our issues will decrease—their payouts are the same, but new investors will have to pay more for the same payout. (Higher share price results in a lower yield and vice versa, as with bonds.)

This provides closed-end fund investors with a major advantage over their mutual fund counterparts. A CEF may for whatever reason—correct or not—fall out of favor, and because of its fixed share count, find its shares trading at a discount to NAV. And this provides the opportunity for investors to purchase it on sale and sometimes for even double-digit markdowns! Put another way, when a CEF trades for less than its NAV, you can buy it at a discount. This means you could buy a dollar's worth of assets for just 90 cent, for example. This never happens with a mutual fund or an ETF.

This is basically "free money" because the CEF's underlying assets are constantly marked to market—meaning they're on the books at fair value. If a CEF owns a bond, that bond issue has a current price for which it could be sold immediately to someone else.

So, for example, if a CEF trades at a 10% discount to NAV—that is, you can buy a dollar of the CEF's value for 90 cents—management could theoretically liquidate and cash out and shareholders all get free money (the 10 cents!). Or it can buy back its own shares to close the discount window and boost the share price.

When we buy CEFs at discounts, we investors get two big advantages:

1. Our yield is higher because we are able to buy *more* bonds for the *same* investment dollar. For example, a fund that achieves a 5% yield on its own NAV becomes 5.5% or 5.6% to us buyers at a discount to NAV.

2. We enjoy upside potential as the discount-to-NAV window *closes* (which it frequently does).

We'll highlight examples of each in a minute. First let's note that CEF managers also have a couple of other major advantages over their mutual fund counterparts. While mutual funds tend to buy popular issues that mirror the market, CEF managers usually have wider mandates and longer leashes. A top CEF manager can take advantage of this flexibility to generate better returns than the market.

A savvy closed-end manager can even borrow cheaply and juice returns. CEFs borrow at rates tied to LIBOR (the London Interbank Offered Rate).

LIBOR is a benchmark interest rate at which major global banks lend to one another in the international interbank market for short-term loans. LIBOR, which stands for London Interbank Offered Rate, serves as a globally accepted key benchmark interest rate that indicates borrowing costs between banks. www.investopedia.com

With that international benchmark just above 2%, it's a good CEF living to borrow cheaply and invest for greater return. The "spread" between lower borrowing costs and higher investment results turns already good yields into great ones.

Many of the funds we like *do* use leverage. It's a "no brainer" boost to our payout when they can earn a safe 4% or so for us and borrow sensibly to turn that into 5%+. Or take a safe 6% and turn that into 7% or even 8%.

Three more reasons to buy bond CEFs instead of ETFs

Before we go any further, let's make sure you're not buying popular marketing vehicles by mistake. We need to stick with handpicked CEFs and not be lured by the fancy and frequent advertisements run by the sales wonks promoting their latest ETF.

Be careful how you buy your bonds. The most popular ETF tickers *do* have a few fatal flaws that'll doom you to underperformance at best, or leave you hanging in the event of a market meltdown at worst!

Let's pick on the widely followed and owned iShares iBoxx High Yield Corporate Bond ETF (HYG) as an example. It has attracted nearly $15 *billion* in assets because:

1. It's convenient, as easy to buy as a stock.

2. It's diversified (for better or worse, as we'll see shortly), with 998 individual holdings.

3. It pays 5.3% today.

The accessibility of funds like this appears cute and comfortable enough. But remember, ETFs are marketing products. They are designed to *attract capital for the managers*, not necessarily to earn you a *return on the capital you invest*.

And in 2018, iShares' High Yield Corporate Bond ETF did exactly what its marketing managers intended. It's attracted a boatload of money, paid its dividends, and … *lost* money for shareholders.

HYG: A High Yield Loser

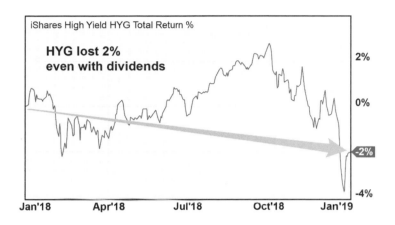

Big money is spent on television, print, and online advertisements for ETFs. Less cash and thought is put into the actual income strategies that ETFs employ, and their lagging returns reflect it.

Let's pick on the three biggest flaws most bond ETFs suffer from. Then, we'll share a superior way to buy bonds via CEFs that is just as easy.

ETF Fatal Flaw #1: Underperformance

Investors who typed in "HYB" instead of "HYG" have typo'd their way to a richer retirement. The CEF New America High Income Fund (HYB) is a way better way to buy high-paying bonds. It has outperformed its ETF cousin by more than 34 percentage points since 2007.

The Smarter CEF Beats Its Popular ETF Cousin

Since its inception 30 years ago, the New America High Income Fund has delivered outstanding returns of 9.5% per year, with investors enjoying most of the fund's returns as cash distributions.

And it still looks like the better play for new money today. The fund pays 8.3% currently, and it trades at a 13.8% discount to the NAV of the bonds it holds. In other words, you can buy it for about 86 cents on the dollar.

The iShares High Yield ETF, meanwhile, pays just 5.3% and trades at "par" to its portfolio—or 100 cents on the dollar. No deal there.

ETF Fatal Flaw #2: Ranking the Worst First

"Passive" methods—building portfolios based on rules—don't work well in the land of bonds because fixed-income expertise can't be readily preprogrammed. And while it's so rare as to be nearly impossible in equity mutual funds, top CEF bond fund managers can and do deliver truly top returns!

Here's the main reason why bond indexing is bad. Let's consider stock indexes, which are weighted by company size. Generally speaking, the larger the firm, the more it matters in the index's performance.

If you "buy by size" in the debt markets, it's counterproductive. Stock market value for indexes doesn't include debt. But bond markets are *all debt by definition*. Follow the computers in Bond-ville and you'd maximize your exposure to the bonds of the firms that borrow the *most* money!

That's the opposite of what we're looking for in bonds, where our goal is to maximize our "coupon" (the percentage yield) while minimizing our risk (and making sure we get paid back our principal).

Let's pick on iShares' High Yield Corporate Bond fund again. Its sixth largest holding is Sprint (S) bonds that expire in September 2023. Will this highly indebted telecom dodge bankruptcy until these coupons expire? Perhaps. This is the type of decision that I'd trust to a human manager (such as at New America) rather than a computer (at iShares).

ETF Fatal Flaw #3: False Sense of Liquidity

And here's the "market meltdown" kicker on why you should always avoid bond ETFs: *They are subject to meltdowns if panic selling occurs.*

Here's why. If you sell the iShares fund today, you'll get your money in exchange for your shares. And it will be iShares' problem to settle up its end (by selling those Sprint bonds and more).

Problem is, we're talking about bonds rather than stocks here, and there is no readily available liquid market for that Sprint paper. Which means if a lot of selling occurs, the iShares ETF itself may take a hit if it has to unload its bonds at a discount (say, 70 or 80 cents on the dollar) to meet investors' withdrawals.

CEFs like the New America High Income Fund don't have this problem. They have *fixed* pools of assets, which help their managers ride out ups and downs. So long as we hire the best managers, who buy good bonds that are funded by reliable cash flows, we (and they) are fine.

CEFs are the underappreciated darling of savvy income investors. They are better bond bets for three reasons:

1. They are actively managed by pros with a legitimate "edge";

2. Their asset pools are fixed, which means they can (and do) trade at discounts to their net asset values, giving us safety and upside; and

3. They can borrow money cheaply, which helps them lever up returns with minimal risk.

Add up these edges, and we have a superior long-term vehicle for fixed-income returns, and we can buy them at a discount by being patient income-seeking contrarians. This means we can do even better than the 9.5% that a fund like New America provided over three decades by "cherry-picking" our purchases.

The Upside of Stocks from Bonds

Dividends made up the bulk of these profits, of course, but the New America CEF rarely yielded 9.5%. The rest came from price upside, which provided investors with a nice kicker and a margin of safety to boot.

For bond funds, upside can come in two ways. First, when the price of a fund lags its net asset value, there is a "discount window" which could subsequently narrow or close. A buyer pays, say, $0.90 for $1.00 of actual investment value (who wouldn't do that all day long?). We specifically target funds when they are unfairly out of favor and have big discounts so that we can profit when investors realize these windows are open too wide.

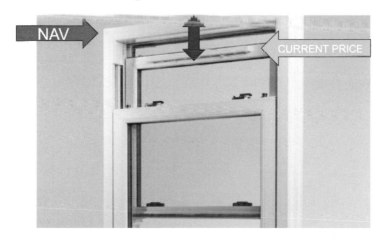

Funds can also gain when NAV itself increases. This means the "liquidation value" of the fund—the value of the bonds, stocks, options, or whatever financial instruments it holds—goes up.

These upside drivers also provide us with a margin of safety on our investment. When it comes to income investing, the best defense is the best offense. You can't keep a good dividend payer down—especially when it's underpriced today.

This is exactly what happened when we purchased PIMCO's Dynamic Credit and Mortgage Fund (PCI). Not only did our subscribers and clients collect the fund's generous dividend (which ranged between 8% and 9%+), but we won two more ways when its:

1. NAV increased (bottom line below), and

2. Its discount window tightened as its price (top line) caught up with—and eventually surpassed—its NAV.

Two Ways to Win for 68% Total Returns

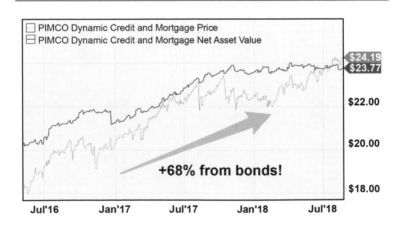

We earned 68% total returns (and counting) from this

PIMCO fund in just two-plus years thanks to the distributions we've collected, the NAV gains we've enjoyed, and the discount window closing entirely—and flipping to a premium!

For much of Dynamic Credit and Mortgage's run, we recommended buying this CEF as long as its "triple threat" potential remained in place. Not only did we call a great run in this fund, but we also "pounded the table" to buy the dips too.

Our Buy Ratings to Date on PCI

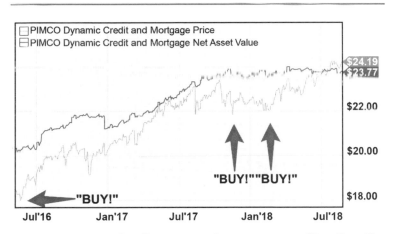

For a period of time in between our "buy" calls, Dynamic Credit was cruising along as a "hold" for us. This happened after its price rallied so furiously that its discount window, for a period of time, closed completely.

When this occurs, we hold, collect the monthly dividend, and wait for our next buying opportunity. That's exactly what happened with Dynamic Credit. Its NAV continued to head *higher* while its price dropped *lower*—which triggered another buying opportunity late last year.

When a fund rallies to too rich a premium to NAV— when we're paying, say, $1.10 for a $1.00 of actual investments (why would we do that?)—we sell it. That's what we did in 2018 when we banked 41% total returns on the Nuveen NASDAQ 100 Dynamic Overwrite Fund (QQQX). The fund became too popular with the first-level types, rallying quickly from a discount to an aggressive premium.

Swings to Premiums Often Provide Extra Profits

CEFs provide better bargains because they have a fixed pool of shares. While mutual funds and ETFs simply issue more shares any time they want, the restricted supply of CEF shares means that their prices trade like stocks.

That's a good thing for us—it means their prices can stray from their underlying net asset values. These big discounts present buying opportunities for us contrarians. Instead of buying bonds directly, the canny CEF investor can scoop up fundamentally sound, cheap, and diversified portfolios of bonds with large yields.

Again, this isn't available to most investors because they only consider mutual funds and ETFs. But that isn't the best way to buy bonds. Now, of course, not all CEFs are born equal and are always good buys. You need to be able to sift through the herd and select the best ones on offer.

This all begins with selecting the right CEF manager.

When it comes to CEFs, you need an active manager

Why are we talking about expensive Lamborghini fund managers in an age of passive and robo investing? After all, we know the massive drag fees can have on portfolio returns. Simply, bonds are different—and this is why.

Information is readily available about thousands of publicly-traded companies. We can buy their stocks easily because they are very liquid—so many shares trade that it's easy to buy and sell. A good thing is that investors can choose from among many companies whose products they use and likely not get burned. Not so for bonds.

The bond market is opaque. Far fewer bonds trade and information is much harder to obtain. This is one reason that bond salespeople are more like the stock brokers of old, who would woo investors with all sorts of tales to encourage buying and selling and, of course, big commissions. (Just read Michael Lewis's delightful *Liar's Poker* about that world!) With the deregulation of stock market commissions, advent of low-cost online discount brokers, and easy information, the shady stock market practices of old are fewer—though not gone. Not so with bonds.

Bond index funds can help, but just as with index funds such as the Vanguard Real Estate ETF (VNQ), their lack of individual selection means the dividend yield is...average or mediocre. But where an astute investor can apply certain principles to select good REITs (real estate investment trusts), there is just no way we are going to succeed with bonds, whether analyzing them for investment or buying and selling them.

We want higher yields than average and we need expertise to snare them. Unlike slogging through thousands of stock funds to find any with active managers who deliver excellent returns, which John Bogle has shown us is almost impossible, there are a few extraordinary bond fund managers we can identify. *If we can find them, they're worth it, because we'll earn much more in higher yields than the extra fee.*

Lucky for us, some of the best professional bond managers have chosen the CEF structure. This lets us buy shares of CEFs whose tip-top managers sift through stacks of available deals to find the best for us. Industry-leading firms like PIMCO, Nuveen, and AllianceBernstein have access to fixed-income opportunities that we regular investors never see. Remember, the bond market is not as democratic and accessible as the stock market.

Let's look at how we go about choosing the best CEF managers to manage your money.

To summarize so far:

1) When looking at charts, remember to add in dividend distributions to calculate overall returns (the price alone may not look exciting, but the distributions can make them so);

Distributions Make a 340% Difference

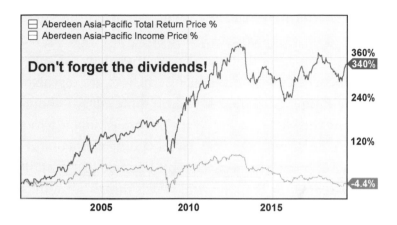

2) You need to go active and select fund managers to manage your CEF investments.

Now we can move on to how you go about choosing the best CEFs for your portfolio.

How to find the best CEFs

We follow some simple rules when selecting which CEFs to invest in. This is what separates our returns from those of first-level thinkers. If you apply these rules when you choose your CEFs, you will be well ahead of most other investors, and so will your returns.

Only buy CEFs that offer above-average yields

You need to demand "alpha." This means that manage-ment is actually adding value beyond what a passive fund or the market provides. After all, you are paying for performance.

Past performance can be an educational indicator of the quality of the management team and its strategy. We look for those managers that have a proven strategy for generating above-average returns that we believe are repeatable into the future. They must also have some edge—whether it's sector knowledge or simply inside connections—to outperform the increasingly "passive" investing world of ETFs.

That edge must be a sustainable one. We invest in dividend streams for the long run, which means we want to own the funds of firms that have the inside track in the fixed-income world.

Take Paul DeNoon, for example. He started with AllianceBernstein, a 50-year-old global investment management firm, in 1992. He leads its Global High Income Fund (AWF). How do we know Paul and his team are good? This fund has an amazing four-fold edge over the S&P 500 since 2000 (returning 754% versus 156%, including distributions). The fund's 10%+ annual returns for its 25-year history demonstrate the quality of the managers investing its assets. And we believe Paul's edge will stay sharp and the fund outperform in years ahead.

Better Call Paul: Safe Bonds Crush Risky Stocks

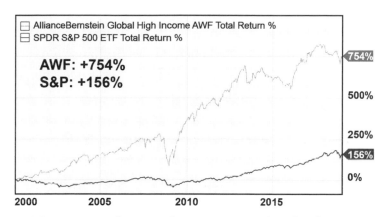

This sustained outperformance signals a fund manager we want looking after our money. And top professionals like Paul are hard to find. Here's another.

Jeffrey Gundlach is the CEO and a founder of Double-Line Capital, an investment management firm with over $120 billion under management. He's recognized as a bond expert, which is probably putting it too lightly. We refer to him as the "bond god" instead.

When we buy or recommend one of his funds, we're hiring Gundlach to be our bond expert. He's picking his favorite emerging market buys, corporate issues, mortgage-backed securities, bank loans, commercial mortgages, collateral loan obligations, and even municipal bonds.

His buys are driven by a sophisticated strategy that shouldn't be replicated at home by you or me. He mostly purchases bonds that are below investment grade or not rated at all (sometimes as much as 80% of his portfolio).

This is, as we've stressed, where the best value is because run-of-the-mill managers and investors avoid these issues. But it takes the very rare savant with substantial know-how to navigate the high-yield bond world successfully.

Since its inception in June 2010, his firm's core fixed-income fund has outpaced its benchmark—the Barclays Aggregate Bond Index—by an incredible 65 percentage points. And that's just the vanilla version of Gundlach's brilliance, which DoubleLine successfully markets to stodgy pension funds (who are handcuffed to investment-grade issues).

But with the DoubleLine Income Solutions Fund (DSL), Gundlach has the freedom to buy anything he wants, anywhere he wants, for any duration he wants. Which is exactly what *we* want—the bond god himself, unshackled and trading for us. And here he is, crushing popular high-yield bond ETFs.

Bond God's CEF Crushes Popular Bond ETFs

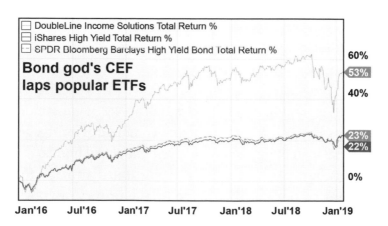

And today, DoubleLine Income Solutions is *still* offering

a 9.7% yield net of fees. That's an unbelievable payout in today's world.

Look at the fund's portfolio mix

If you are going to achieve serious returns, then you need to be investing with managers that know how to play in the so-called "sub-investment" end of the market.

The best deals in the corporate bond market are actually just below the somewhat arbitrary investment grade cut-off. It's where savvy fund managers and second-level investors like us capitalize on the fact that the overly cautious by-laws of pension funds, banks, and insurance companies prohibit investing in these "low quality" (according to the herd, but not to us) issues. They are handcuffed to investment-grade bonds—hence the investment-grade price premiums.

They can't shop where we do, which means more room in the aisles for us! This is where Paul goes shopping, on the fringe of the investment-grade aisle—where bond bargains are found.

The secret is to buy bonds the big money isn't allowed to.

To illustrate the point further, let's look at the Black-Rock Floating Rate Income Strategies Fund (FRA), which buys floating-rate debt. (More about floating-rate debt in a moment). For now, just know that most of the bonds it buys are issued by corporations, and most of them are below the "investment grade" demarcation.

It doesn't matter what a rating agency says. What matters more is the actual health of a business, its cash flow, and its ability to service its debt.

BlackRock's managers David Delbos, Mitchell Garfin, and Josh Tarnow take advantage of the absence of big buyers in these debt pools. Delbos, Garfin, and Tarnow love the Bs—they've got 94% of the portfolio in BBB-, BB-, or B-rated debt. Have a look at the makeup of their portfolio at the end of 2018.

FRA Finds Value in "B List" Bonds

Type	Fund	■ Type
AAA Rated	0.2%	
AA Rated	0.6%	I
A Rated	0.8%	I
BBB Rated	5.0%	■■
BB Rated	29.7%	■■■■■■■■■
B Rated	59.1%	■■■■■■■■■■■■■■■
CCC Rated	3.8%	■
CC Rated	0.4%	I
Not Rated	3.4%	■
Cash and/or Derivatives	-3.0%	■

When selecting your CEFs, this is the type of portfolio mix you are looking for—light on the investment grades and weighted to the Bs. This is where the managers really earn their fees.

By the way, like the DoubleLine fund, BlackRock's Floating Rate Income Strategies has also outperformed popular high-yield ETFs over the last 10 years.

It Pays to Play the Bs

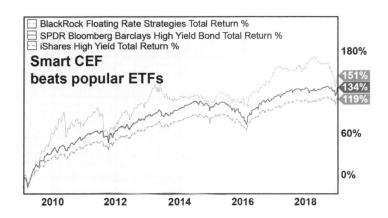

When you back an experienced management team, you can take comfort that they are selecting specific companies with stable cash flows (to pay the debt) and high-quality collateral (in case the cash flows disappoint).

The BlackRock fund currently holds a mix of 527 holdings across various industries. They're mostly issued by domestic companies, with 94% based in the US and Canada, stable jurisdictions with great diversification where any one "failure" will have minimal impact on the overall portfolio.

Have a look at a fund's fact sheets (available on its website) to see what the investment portfolio looks like. AllianceBernstein's Paul DeNoon, like our favorite bond gurus, doesn't mess around with highly graded debt because it's difficult to find value there. Only 12% of his portfolio is stashed in AAA-, AA-, and A-rated debt (investment grade is AAA, AA, A, or BBB). This is one way to know you've got the right manager.

Buy CEFs where there is inside share ownership

Fund managers that back themselves with their personal funds on the line are worth looking at.

Turning back to the AllianceBernstein example, Paul and his team *know* they are good too. He owns 65,000 shares of the Global High Income Fund in his personal account. And Douglas Feebles, Chief Investment Officer of AB's fixed-income division, owns 40,000 shares. This level of insider confidence is a rare, bullish sign in the CEF world, where fewer than half of funds have *any* insider ownership.

Have a look at insider share ownership when selecting your CEFs. It speaks volumes of the confidence you can place in the management team.

Only buy CEFs that trade at a discount

We always demand a discount. And so should you. As we've described above, this is a feature unique to CEFs— thanks to their fixed number of shares, they can (and often do) trade at discounts to their net asset value. Our reasoning for this is twofold:

1. Few funds deserve a premium,

2. And those that do can usually, eventually, be purchased at a discount anyway.

Don't let any first-level investor tell you that the price you pay doesn't matter if you're investing for dividends. Price always matters.

Here's a real-life example from 2016. Let's compare two

bond funds. Both paid big 10%+ yields. Both benefited from a brilliant bond manager at the helm.

In fact, they shared the same manager—Jeffrey Gundlach.

And both funds shared a "wide mandate" that basically gave Gundlach and his team the go-ahead to buy anything they wanted. The only difference between the two funds was price per asset owned. The DoubleLine Opportunistic Credit Fund (DBL) traded for a 17% premium to its net asset value, while the DoubleLine Income Solutions Fund traded for a 7% discount to NAV.

In other words, investors were paying $1.17 for just $1 in assets for Gundlach's first fund, while paying only $0.93 on the dollar for the assets in his second fund. And there didn't seem to be any good reason for the discrepancy, other than perhaps unlucky timing for the launch of the second fund.

We say unlucky for Gundlach, but lucky for investors looking to pick up a wonderful opportunity giving investors who jumped in at the time to grab up to a 7% upside.

From late 2013 through the start of 2018, first-level investors fretted about the possibility of higher interest rates. Thanks to these worries, early investors were able to purchase DoubleLine's Income Solutions at a 7% discount, for a total 11% yield.

Investors who purchased then earned a 33% total return (including dividends) over 13 months! Meanwhile, investors who overpaid for DoubleLine Opportunistic Credit, the sister fund, saw their money go nowhere.

The Difference? The Discount

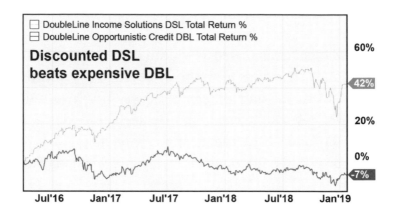

DoubleLine Opportunistic Credit continued to pay its same monthly dividend, just as you'd expect. Its investors, however, suffered a "lost year" simply because they over-paid for the fund.

As we mentioned earlier in this chapter, it's no coincidence that CEFs trading for big discounts *also* offer out-sized yields. Here's why.

When funds set their distributions, they do so as a percentage of their current asset base. Just as you think of your retirement withdrawals as a percentage of *your* over-all portfolio, a CEF sets its distribution on the value of *its* portfolio.

But there's one big difference—its portfolio can some-times trade at a discount to its fair value. And you and we as income investors can often secure the best deal by *waiting* and buying these funds *only when their assets are trading at a discount.*

Which means we get the same payout, and we pay even

less for it. Our yield is higher than it would be in an otherwise rational investment world. We get more dividend for our dollar.

Of course, there's no guarantee that a cheap fund won't get cheaper in the short term. But over time, the market will normalize and discounted funds will see their prices trend up toward their underlying NAVs. Fund managers can even force the appreciation by buying back their own shares, which we'll discuss shortly.

Learn to love watching these closed-end fund discounts because they're clear contrarian indicators. The more investors dislike a strategy now, the greater the discount they demand. The irony is that most people love chasing recent performance, which means they're most inclined to sell a loser at the moment it's most likely to turn around.

Be careful of CEFs trading at a premium to NAV

The other side of the coin is those CEFs trading at a premium to NAV. Aggressive investors chasing big-name funds are willing to pay a premium. For example, recent buyers of PIMCO's excellent (but overpriced) Global StocksPLUS & Income Fund (PGP) paid $1.48 per dollar in assets. Why would you overpay for a dollar at the bank?

Top-notch managers' fund prices often exceed NAV. Investors are willing to pay more than $1 for a dollar in assets for the managers' future performance just to get in today. That happens a lot for PIMCO funds. In fact, two more PIMCO funds round out our "most overpriced" list.

4 Popular Premiums to Avoid

FUND	PREMIUM	COST FOR $1 IN ASSETS
PIMCO Global StocksPLUS (PGP)	48%	$1.48
PIMCO Strategic Income Fund (RCS)	42%	$1.42
PIMCO High Income Fund (PHK)	39%	$1.39
Gabelli Utility Trust (GUT)	31%	$1.31

Paying a premium might make sense if you are buying a growth stock, but it's the wrong approach to income investing. We don't have to "buy and hope" for growth. We can snare amazing yields and price upside when we buy cheaply, without the risk that "hopes" will be dashed.

That's why we always demand a discount from any CEF we buy. Our yield is higher than it would be if the fund traded for NAV (because income is earned per NAV unit, so the less we pay for it, the better).

Paying a premium for a fund is the opposite of buying it at a discount. Instead of buying $1.00 for just $0.90, you're paying $1.10. And personally, we prefer not to be down 10% out of the gate. Neither should you.

Get your management fee "comped"

Another advantage of buying at a discount? When the discount is greater than the management fee—and we don't buy if it isn't!—we in effect pay *zero* management fee.

Let the first-level investor types waste time over which dumb computer-driven fund pays the least. You and I can pay a well-connected bond manager *nothing* while we lock in 8%+ yields with big upside when we buy their funds at a discount to NAV.

Let's go back to the DoubleLine Income Solutions Fund. On the face of it, it may appear that Gundlach's 1.44% management fee for DoubleLine Income Solutions is expensive—but it's actually a *bargain*. Most investors are conditioned by their experience with mutual funds and ETFs to search out the lowest fees, almost to a fault. This makes sense for investment vehicles that are roughly going to perform in line with the broader market. Passive index investing is the way to go there, no argument (Vanguard's late great Jack Bogle won that one!). Lowering your costs minimizes performance drag.

CEFs are a different investment animal, though. Overall, there are many more dogs than gems. As we've emphasized, it's an absolute necessity to find a great manager with a solid track record. The very select few who exist aren't cheap. We wouldn't, however, pay a *premium* to invest with anyone, even Gundlach. But we will pay 1.44% for him and DoubleLine Income Solutions if the expense fee is "comped," because it's less than the fund's discount to NAV.

DoubleLine Income Solutions is trading at a discount of 4.4% to NAV. Now compare that to its fee of 1.44%, and you can see how you are getting the "bond god" to work for you for free, and even better, he's netting you nearly 3% in free assets. And this is without the monthly dividends. This is why we say the fee is "comped."

Plus, it's important to remember that all yields that you see quoted are *net of fees*, which means that DoubleLine's

9.7% current yield already has the bond god's cut sub-
tracted from it.

While we love to invest in CEFs offering a discount
to NAV and actively seek out those offering at least a 5%
discount, we don't simply buy every big discount we see.
Just as with dividend-paying stocks, we search under every
bush for the very best CEFs.

Watch out for discount traps

A steep discount is a great start, but many funds underperform—or worse, lose their investors' money—over the
long haul because they have no means to close that discount
window. Not every manager is a bond rock star, after all, or
can count on investors eventually flocking to them, so we
can't count on price appreciation from closing a window—
if it's going to be stuck open. Some funds stay in the discount doghouse forever. The popular BlackRock Resources
& Commodity Fund (BCX) trades at a 10%+ discount today,
but for good reason—it never makes its shareholders any
money!

Worse than a Piggy Bank

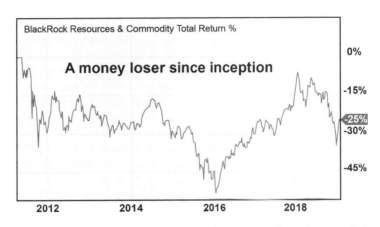

As a result, its discount window stays "stuck open" for years on end. Let's see why this is.

Investors Aren't Rushing to Scoop Up This Discount

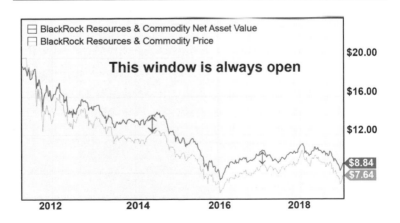

Notice the gap between the two lines for the BlackRock Resources & Commodity CEF. This fund's price always

lags its NAV by about 10 cents on the dollar. Christmas—
price gains from price closing in on NAV—never comes.
Cheap closed-end funds are no different from cheap stocks.
"Value" investing itself is simply no guarantee of gains. (We
suspect you know this, having smartly found your way to
dividend payers, but it's worth repeating!) Sometimes securities are cheap for a reason, the so-called "value trap."

As a second-level investor, you will know to look for
underlying reasons for any discount. And if you go back
over time and see that the discount window has never
closed, exercise caution. It may be stuck—and your money
will be too.

Where is the dividend being paid from?

Here's another catch. Some funds pay big distributions
that look great—but they're not sustainable. However, they
continue to attract new (sucker) investors because they are
able to fund their payouts. They just happen to shed their
NAV at a similar pace!

For example, here are two more CEF dogs that have lost
money for the last five years (even when accounting for
dividends paid) at the same time the S&P 500 has soared.

Big Yields, but Lackluster Returns

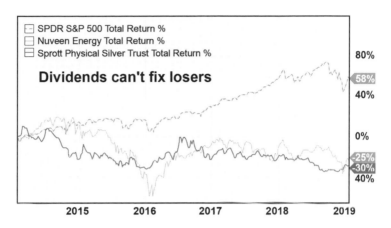

Why'd these funds get trounced by the broader market? They simply didn't generate enough income from their portfolios or enough gains from their holdings. Remember, a closed-end fund can pay us from some combination of:

1. Investment income,

2. Capital gains, and/or

3. Return of capital.

Of the three, investment income is preferable because it's usually the most reliable. Many CEFs pay monthly distributions, so it's best if they match up their payouts with steady income streams. Yes, capital gains from rising bond or stock prices can further boost distributions, but they are risky. To get the cash from a gain, the fund has to sell the bond or stock. When markets turn south, those gains on paper can disappear just when the CEF needs them to fund distributions. Plus, capital gains aren't guaranteed.

That leads to the bottom line. If distributions are unsus-tainable—if they require taking investment gains (which are uncertain at best) to survive—they might be reduced or cut. And while most CEF investors are used to some varia-tion in bond fund payouts, a big cut means the price of the CEF will plummet. That's the real bummer.

Closing the discount window

Now that you are aware of some common pitfalls and have decided on a CEF that has a "legitimate" discount to NAV, you'll want to be able to identify one or more catalysts that are likely to propel any price gains. A "catalyst" in the market is just like a catalyst in chemistry class: something that makes an event happen. What could close the window?

Fund managers have three ways to close discount win-dows: good performance, stock repurchases, and paying dividends out of capital (which, despite what we've just written, can be justified in rare cases).

Good performance is the first "must have." But in a world where the "bond god" Gundlach himself can run an undercover fund (see DoubleLine Income Solutions), it's no guarantee that new money will come knocking over-night and boost the price.

Fortunately, savvy CEF management teams have two more tools available at their disposal. CEF buybacks (repur-chasing its own stock on the open market), when executed at opportune times, are gifts that keep giving. Not only do they help close the window, but they *also boost NAV per share* as stock is removed from the market.

In addition to repurchases, there's one more technique a savvy management team can use successfully. They pay dividends out of existing capital when the window is especially wide.

At a glance, this looks bad. Many investors believe that CEF distributions should always be fully funded from investment income because they think of corporate dividends (which are indeed best funded by profits). So "distributions from income" may sound like a safe analogy, but it will actually make you miss out on the best opportunities.

For example, let's say we ran a fund trading at a 17% discount to NAV. We could make some quick money simply by taking our fund private (buying it out) for $0.83 on the dollar and then selling the assets for $1 on the dollar.

Or if we didn't want to close the fund, we could simply find a way to close the discount window. Paying dividends from capital is one way to do this. Think of this as partially taking the fund private—by returning some initial money to investors (lowering the NAV) as a way to force the discount window to shut a bit.

And now on to changing interest rates, another major concern. You might think that savvy CEF managers, equipped with MacGyver-esque toolkits and wide mandates, have an answer for rising rates. If so, you'd be right.

CHAPTER 5

Safe High-Yield CEFs in Any Rate Environment

EVEN IN TODAY'S low interest rate environment, you can find some quality CEFs yielding 8%. This means if you have a million dollars invested, you're earning $80,000 annually in dividends alone—without having to sell any principal.

Compare that salary with your friends who instead invest in "safe" Treasury bills and bonds. Your nest egg is generating more than twice as much income as their measly 2.8%!

And we can further improve on our No Withdrawal retirement strategy by buying stocks and funds when they are out of favor. Not only do we secure outsized yields when we purchase with a contrarian mindset, but we can also enjoy upside as prices normalize and the discount window closes. That can bring us total returns beyond 8% a year, with reduced risk!

If this all sounds so good, you may ask why investors currently ignore the benefits of a CEF investment. What is the catch?

In a word, the Fed. The Federal Reserve has been a headline worry for CEFs ever since we started buying them in 2015 for our portfolios and recommending them to sub-scribers and clients.

We say "headline" in jest because few financial outlets talk about these funds—let alone make them headlines in their articles—and even fewer talk about them intelli-gently. Which is just fine with us income seekers. The lack of broader attention presents us with opportunity. And the few pundits that do write about CEFs from time to time usually warn—wrongly—that the sector will be negatively affected by rising rates for two reasons.*

CEF Rate Fear #1: Leverage (Borrowing) Will Become Costly

As we've already described, closed-end fund managers can borrow cheaply and improve returns by earning more than the cost of borrowing. But the most common borrow-ing rate we know is LIBOR, and that benchmark is closely tied to the fed funds rate. So, the thinking goes, higher fed rates will end the "cheap money" party that benefits CEFs.

> Leverage: If you buy a house with 10% down and get a loan for the rest, you are 90% leveraged. If your down payment is 20%, your leverage is 80%. As we learned during the housing crisis, leverage is great on the way up and can be painful on the way down. CEFs which use 20% to 33% leverage are, in general, being very prudent, improving potential returns but not betting the farm.

---

*   As we went to print, the Federal Reserve was leaning towards additional rate hikes. But rate outlooks change as quickly as Western New York's weather (where we both proudly grew up). Consider this chapter a playbook for any rising rate cycle. When rate expectations are trending lower, you'll want to emphasize fixed-rate bond funds, which we'll dis-cuss afterwards.

Many of the funds we own and recommend use 20% to 33% leverage. It's a "no brainer" boost to our payout when they can earn a safe 6% or so for us and turn that into 8%+ by using leverage. If that leverage became too expensive—if interest rates jumped—our funds would be forced to cut back on their debt and, most importantly to us, their distributions.

But how costly is "too costly?"

More than most armchair analysts think, and rates are unlikely to get to these "breaking point" levels for CEFs. Why? We simply look at the past. During the last rate hike cycle, from 2004 to 2006, prominent CEFs did just fine. Let's first consider the tax-advantaged Nuveen AMT-Free Muni Credit Fund (NVG), which rose in harmony with Alan Greenspan's fed funds rate.

Higher Rates No Problem for Muni Bonds Then

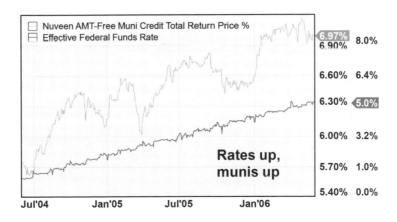

And *this* rate hike cycle, we can simply update the months and years to see a similar picture.

Higher Rates No Problem for Muni Bonds Now

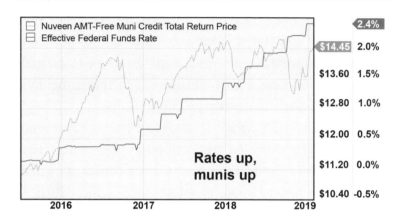

Other types of CEFs were also able to perform well in the face of rising rates. Here are two more of our favorites during the 2004–2006 rate hike cycle.

Rising Rates No Problem for CEFs

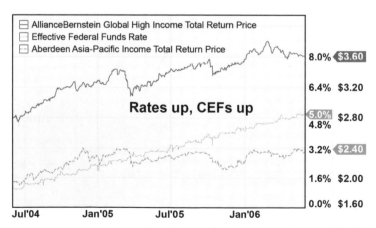

As you can see in this chart, the last time the Fed hiked rates significantly, CEFs did just fine. And we mean "significantly" as in from 1% to 5.25%. That was a real-life stress test for CEFs. Yet perennial No Withdrawal favorites AllianceBernstein's Global High-Income Fund (AWF) and Aberdeen's Asia-Pacific Income Fund (FAX) all outperformed the broader market during this two-year span! (They delivered 30% and 23% total returns including dividends versus 19% for the S&P 500.)

So we believe you have plenty of cost-of-borrowing runway to continue buying CEFs and banking their dividends. And even if we're wrong about rates staying relatively low for quite some time, you'll have years to decades to monitor and re-evaluate—if and when the fed funds rate ever hits 5% again.

But are we missing something by focusing only on short term rates? Let's now consider the 10 year Treasury, which is the crux of the second argument from the uninformed "CEF caution" crowd. They say that when long-dated Treasuries pay more, rival "bond proxies" such as CEFs will be less attractive. Perhaps, but how much more would "more" have to be?

CEF Rate Fear #2: More High-Paying Competition

Simply put, long-dated Treasuries haven't paid enough to damper CEFs in at least two decades.

This time around, the yield of the 10-year Treasury— the benchmark long bond—has risen from a post-World War II low of under 1.4% to its current still-near-historical nadir of 2.8%. Here's a 55-year chart to bring that home. Let's zoom in on the microscopic uptick in the lower-right of this chart—the bump from 1.4% to 2.8%.

The Long View of the 10-Year Bond

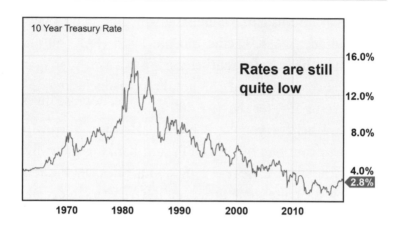

This perspective shows that the "competition" argument was, and remains, ridiculous. An 8% yield still looks pretty darned good in a 3% world. This is why we believe CEFs should be able to handle higher short- and long-term interest rates without a problem. And it is doubtful that either rate will reach those levels this cycle. This means we're probably clear for five or 10 years *or more*. (And if we're wrong about this, we have *plenty* of runway between now and then to revisit it.)

And finally, the mainstream media and the internet are allergic to this type of actual analysis. The two "fears" we debunked are stated so often that they are accepted as common knowledge. But we haven't seen either challenged.

It's time to move on to how you make sure you're buying the right types of bonds. We've already touched on the rising-rate cycle, and we'll go into it in more detail now. It's important that you know why short- and long-term yields are rising—and then how to invest accordingly.

Floating on air with floating-rate bonds

What happens to the 10-year Treasury paying 3% if rates rally to 4%? Your old bond loses value, because investors prefer the new bond (with the higher-paying coupon). After all, you signed up for a decade!

For example, if you buy a 10-year Treasury bond today, you're getting more or less a mere 3%. Your interest payments are secure, but your principal is at risk as rates continue to rise. Is that because, as everyone knows, bond prices always move in the opposite direction of interest rates?

Not exactly. Sure, nobody will want your 3% bond if they can buy a newer, better issue yielding 3.5% or 4%. But your problem isn't the fact that you own a bond. Your problem is that its *fixed rate* no longer looks as good as it used to.

Floating-rate bonds don't have this problem. They have variable coupons (interest payments) that are calculated quarterly, or even monthly. Their rates take some reference rate, such as the federal funds rate, and add a defined payout percentage to it. As the reference rate ticks higher, so does the coupon's payout.

There are now two reputable ETF options for Treasury investors who want the adjustable rates: the iShares Treasury Floating Rate Bond ETF (TFLO) and the WisdomTree Bloomberg Floating Rate Treasury ETF (USFR). Both are designed to perform better than fixed-rate Treasuries when the Fed is hiking interest rates.

But that's a function of *not losing* money rather than *producing meaningful yield*—our goal. Since their inception in February 2014, the Treasury Floating Rate Bond ETF and WisdomTree Bloomberg CEF have produced a total return of 3.4% and 2.8%, respectively. They may be geared for good *relative* performances with respect to Treasuries, but their *absolute* performances are awful. We want better.

Instead of investing in these barely cash equivalents, we prefer corporate debt.

We need to pick the right companies, of course, to make sure we get paid back. But if we smartly target companies with stable (and preferably, growing) cash flows, we can earn ourselves a nice premium to stodgy old Treasuries without taking on much extra risk. Plus, many corporate bonds have floating-rate components—which means we can put together a bond portfolio that is geared to perform well during any rate environment (rising, declining, or steady).

First-level investors instinctively look to ETFs that meet our "floating corporate" criteria. And the VanEck Vectors Investment Grade Floating Rate ETF (FLTR) buys floating-rate notes from businesses that are rated as investment grade by Moody's, S&P, or Fitch. It currently pays a paltry 2.6%.

Slightly Better than Your Mattress

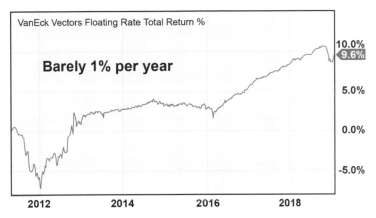

The VanEck fund has delivered a *total* return to investors of just 9.6% since inception nearly seven years ago. That's barely more than 1% each year. Yikes.

At this point you won't be surprised to learn that floating-rate bond CEFs are our go-to instrument when the Fed is in a hiking mood, but we have to be choosy.

Bonds that rise with rates—floating-rate corporate bond funds

One of our favorite CEF managers is Scott Page. He's been with Eaton Vance, one of the oldest investment management firms in the US, since 1989. He has conducted the Eaton Vance Floating-Rate Income Trust (EFT, not to be confused with ETF, an exchange-traded fund) brilliantly since inception—through rising and falling rate cycles, through rising and falling stock markets.

Funds like Eaton Vance's Floating-Rate Income Trust tend to deliver on their promised distributions and price upside when rates rise. These funds barely blink when stocks plummet, and they even hold steady when rates plummet.

The secret? They buy corporate bonds. These issues have higher yields and more flexibility than, say, US Treasuries. As rates move higher, these money managers aren't left with has-been pieces of paper. They can cycle into higher-paying investments, and Scott does this. His loans, on average, reset every 48 days. Thanks to a portfolio that features 90% floating-rate loans, he isn't stranded if rates spike. He simply rides the rate wave to higher payments.

When the bonds mature, Scott will simply roll the capital into new corporate bonds. He can search the public and private markets for deals (showing another advantage of bonds over stocks—the universe is larger). And if interest rates are higher then, he'll capture the higher yield.

It's a simple formula. During rate hike periods, you want to own the best floating-rate funds because they steadily grind higher.

Riding the Fed Wave to Floating-Rate Returns

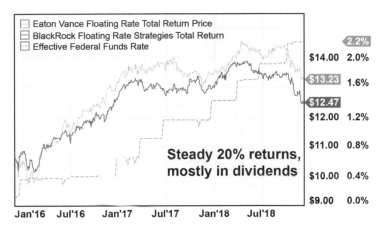

Eaton Vance's Floating-Rate Income Trust and Black-Rock's Floating Rate Income Strategies Fund averaged 20% returns from December 1, 2015, to December 1, 2018 (while the Fed was hiking its target rate). Most of these gains came in the form of monthly cash distributions. The two funds yielded 5% to 6% annually or more during this entire time.

As we write, there are questions about whether or not the current rate hike cycle is closer to its end point than its start point. Does this mean we should sell our floating-rate funds and cycle back into fixed-rate offerings?

We have one potential historical parallel we can draw on. In the summer of 2006, when then-Fed chair Alan Greenspan capped off three years of rate hikes, the BlackRock and Eaton Vance funds both continued to rally until the following summer even though rates were going nowhere.

The Fed rate remained unchanged, while the 10-year Treasury rate traded in a range between 4.4% and 5.3%.

Interest rates went nowhere, yet our two floating-rate funds averaged 20% gains in 12 months. Who would have predicted that!

The floating party didn't last forever, of course. These funds peaked soon after the 10-year rate hit its high in the summer of 2007.

Which begs the question: has the 10-year rate peaked? It's too early to tell. Until we see a breakout above 3.2% or a breakdown below 1.5%, we should assume that long rates are also meandering sideways.

10-Year Rate is Rangebound

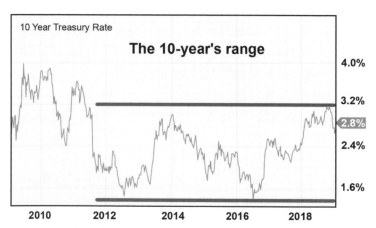

We won't hold these funds forever through all rate-hike cycles. But we should make sure to consider their prices, discounts, and yields when we sell them. Both funds are incredibly cheap and their dividends are well funded. For example, the Floating Rate Income Strategies fund pays 6.2% yet trades at a 13% discount to its NAV. Shares trade for just 87 cents on the dollar, the cheapest they've been in 10 years!

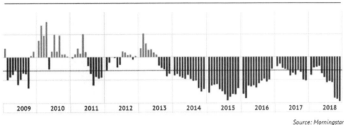

FRA's Historic 13% Discount to NAV

Source: Morningstar

The Eaton Vance Floating-Rate Income Trust, meanwhile, pays 6.3% and offers a 12% discount to its NAV. It hasn't been this cheap since the days after the financial crisis.

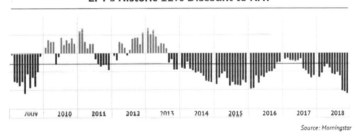

EFT's Historic 12% Discount to NAV

Source: Morningstar

At these prices, we're not going to change our portfolios just yet. But we'll look to balance our bond buying within the context of the unfolding Fed action as we build our secure fixed-income portfolio.

CHAPTER 6

Stock "Hybrids"

AS INVESTORS NEAR retirement, they tend to favor bonds, which provide income and less drama than stocks. However, less drama means less potential upside. With retirees living longer than ever before—which means much more time for inflation to eat away at your nest egg's purchasing power—it's important to not become too conservative too early in life. And fortunately, even 65 or 70 may be too early today!

One suggested solution for our long life expectancy "problem" is to stay with stocks longer. But stocks can go down as well as up, and a big pullback can inflict permanent damage on a portfolio.

So we want to capture the dividends that stocks pay and the upside potential that they provide by minimizing our downside risk. We can do this by focusing on hybrid vehicles that are designed to extract payouts and provide downside buffers. Let's start with an underappreciated way to double your dividends from stocks that you may already own.

Preferred shares: They pay double mere "common" dividends

Not familiar with preferred shares? You're not alone—most investors only consider "common" shares of stock when they look for income. You probably know the problem with this approach. Common stock in S&P 500 companies pays just 2.0% today, on average. But you can double, triple, or even quadruple your yields and actually reduce your risk by trading in your common shares for preferreds.

A company will issue preferred shares to raise capital, just as it offers bonds. In return it will pay regular dividends on these shares and, as the name suggests, preferred shareholders receive their payouts *before* common shares. They typically get paid more, and even have a priority claim over common stock on the company's earnings and assets in case something bad happens, like bankruptcy. They are "preferred" over common stock, and after secured debt, in the bankruptcy pecking order.

So far, so good. The tradeoff? Less upside. But in today's expensive stock market—still pricey even after the late 2018 correction—that may not be a bad substitution to make. Let's walk through a sample common-for-preferred exchange that would nearly double your current dividends with a simple trade-in.

The common shares from JPMorgan Chase (JPM) pay 3.1%. But the firm recently issued Series DD preferreds paying 5.75%. JPMorgan Chase shareholders looking for more income may be happy to make this tradeoff.

Meanwhile, Bank of America (BAC) common pays 2.1% today. But B of A just issued some preferreds that pay a fat 5.88%. That's a 180% potential income raise for share-holders who want to trade in their garden-variety shares. But how exactly do we buy these as individual investors? Which series are we looking for again?

A big problem with preferred shares is that they are complicated to purchase without the help of a human bro-ker. So, many investors attempt to streamline their online buys and simply purchase ETFs that specialize in pre-ferreds, such as the Invesco Preferred ETF (PGX) and the iShares S&P Preferred Stock Index Fund (PFF). After all, these funds pay up to 6.1% and, in theory, they diversify your credit risk. Unfortunately, many ETF buyers have little understanding of preferred shares—let alone how a partic-ular fund invests in them. Should we entrust the selection of preferred shares to a mere formula baked into an ETF?

No! The problem with the ETF model is that it doesn't account for credit risk as accurately as an expert human can. Which means a better idea is—you guessed it—to find an active manager to handpick your preferred portfolio. Buy-ing a discounted closed-end fund is the best way to do this. Here are three preferred CEFs that have all outperformed their more popular ETF cousins over the past five years.

The Top Three Are CEFs, Bottom Two Are ETFs

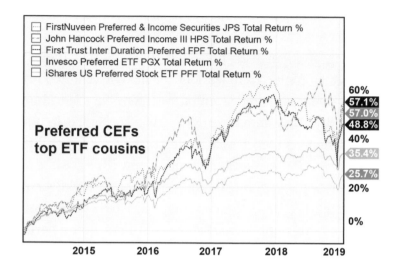

You'll rarely get a deal buying an ETF. They don't trade at discounts because their sponsors simply issue more shares to capitalize on any increased demand. We CEF investors don't have this popularity problem; we can get a deal. We simply wait and only purchase CEFs when they trade at a discount to their net asset values (or the sum of the market prices of the preferred shares they own minus any leverage).

The preferred ETFs, Invesco Preferred and iShares US Preferred, yield 5.8% and 6.1%, respectively, and trade roughly at their "par" value, which means we're paying $1 for $1 in preferred shares. Meanwhile, Nuveen Preferred & Income Securities Fund (JPS), a CEF, yields more (7.5%) and trades for just 96 cents on the dollar! Plus, it has the benefit of an active manager, which is why the fund regularly outperforms its ETF counterparts.

Better Yields, Deals, and Returns with CEFs

TICKER	NAME	FUND TYPE	YIELD	PREMIUM (OR DISCOUNT) TO NAV	5-YEAR RETURN
JPS	Nuveen Preferred & Income Securities Fund	CEF	8.4%	-3.7%	57.1%
HPS	John Hancock Preferred Income Fund	CEF	7.6%	-1.4%	57.0%
FPF	First Trust Intermediate Duration Preferred & Income Fund	CEF	8.2%	-5.9%	48.7%
PFF	iShares US Preferred Stock ETF	ETF	6.1%	0.0%	25.7%
PGX	Invesco Preferred ETF	ETF	5.8%	0.1%	35.4%

When we're shopping in the preferred aisle, it's a "no brainer" to go with the CEF concierge service. They yield more, they appreciate in price more, and best of all, the money manager is *free* when we buy at a discount.

How about a few more preferred ideas? Here are four more excellent funds with managers that'll work for you for free. Today, each of these funds:

- Yields more than 7%,

- Trades at a discount to NAV, and

- Has generated returns of 7% or better on NAV since inception.

TICKER	FUND	YIELD	DISCOUNT TO NAV	RETURN ON NAV SINCE INCEPTION
LDP	Cohen & Steers Ltd Duration Preferreds	8.2%	4.4%	7.9%
FLC	Flaherty & Crumrine Total Return	7.7%	6.9%	7.4%
JPI	Nuveen Preferred & Income Term	7.6%	6.2%	7.8%
FFC	Flaherty & Crumrine Preferred Secs	7.5%	2.1%	7.7%

When it comes to preferred funds, past performance is usually an excellent indicator of future results. As with muni bonds, skills and connections help generate superior returns over the long haul. It's no coincidence that Flaherty & Crumrine runs three of the funds that we highlighted above; the firm is legendary in the preferred space.

Convertible Bonds

Convertible bonds, like preferreds, pay interest. But they are *also* like stock options in that they can be "converted" from a bond to a share of stock by the holder. So you can think of them as bonds with some stock-like upside.

Switching from creditor (owning a bond) to shareholder (owning stock) can be a lucrative move. But buying convertibles *does* require individual research. We prefer to "outsource" this task to experts, and again here, CEFs are our favorite way to buy convertibles.

For example, asset manager Nuveen expanded its Preferred & Income Securities Fund's mandate recently. Along with preferred securities, the fund began buying hybrids such as convertible securities. (The fund started purchasing debt that has options to convert to equity.) We didn't worry about this mandate change because we trusted the management team.

The SPDR Bloomberg Barclays Convertible Bond ETF (CWB) is the most popular mainstream vehicle to purchase convertibles. It lets investors join this "country club" favorite and brag to their friends that they own a basket of convertible bonds. But if their friends are impressed, their accountants are not.

Bloomberg Barclays Convertible Bond has, on the surface, been fine. It's generated 159% returns over the last 10 years. Problem is, its stock market competition—the S&P

500—returned 280%. And its bond market competition, Nuveen Preferred & Income, returned an amazing 317%. Which means that this "country club ETF" blended the two strategies and did worse than both! (All while smart bond buyers were enjoying larger yields, lower risk, and superior total returns with Nuveen Preferred & Income.)

CEF First, Index Second, ETF Last

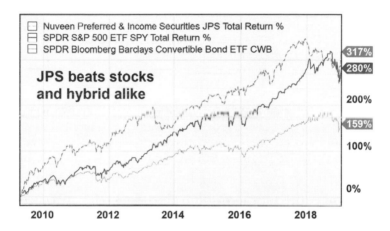

Could we improve upon Bloomberg Barclays Convertible Bond by hiring some smarter management? We do have one "pure play" option in CEF-land that meets our previous criteria for desirable preferred funds. The Ellsworth Growth and Income Fund (ECF) pays 5.9% today, more than double the 2.6% yield of the Bloomberg Barclays fund, and trades at a generous discount to its NAV:

TICKER	FUND	YIELD	DISCOUNT TO NAV	RETURN ON NAV SINCE INCEPTION
ECF	Ellsworth Growth & Income	5.9%	13.8%	6.0%

And, oh, by the way, it's outperformed its too-popular ETF cousin over the past 10 years as well. Including dividends, Ellsworth Growth and Income has generated 203% profits versus 159% for Bloomberg Barclays.

The Convertible CEF: A Superior Ride

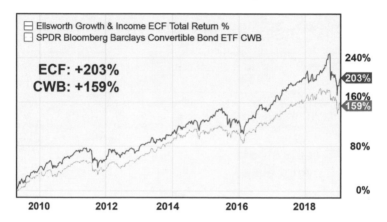

Convertibles promise bond-like returns with stock-like upside, but we're also going to discuss another technique that trades the upside of blue-chip stocks for income in excess of their usual dividends. We're going to write (or sell) covered call options for steady payouts. It's a strategy you may have dabbled in yourself before. It can be time consuming and confusing for individual investors to execute, but don't worry—we've got a one-click way for you to build a portfolio of covered call–powered income. Plus, covered calls don't have the risk usually associated with options trading.

Covered Calls

Most investors *buy* stocks and *hope* they'll go up in price. They do nothing in the interim to generate cash flow from those stocks while they sit in their portfolio. Dividends are a good start in the other direction—the positive direction. But did you know that it's possible to *accelerate* many payouts, to create your own quick dividends, so to speak, by writing covered calls?

"Write" *what?*

To explain, first note that we'll again highlight funds that will generate *10% cash yields or better* from this income strategy without actually handling an options contract yourself.

A *call* option is a contract that gives its buyer the right to *purchase* a stock from the seller for a certain price within a certain period of time. For that right, the buyer pays the seller a sum upfront, called a premium.

Option traders buy calls hoping they can multiply their money in a short period of time. Rather than buy a stock and hope for a 10% gain in a year or so, they buy call options aiming for a 100% gain in a month.

Of course there's a catch—otherwise option traders would be the richest people in the world! And that caveat is *time.* When you buy a call option, not only do you need the share price to move higher for you to make money, but you also need it to happen within a relatively short timeframe. The clock is ticking. Loudly. With each day that passes, options decay in value and are worth less for the buyers. That's bad for them, but great for sellers (those who "write" the call options)—those who collected the premium up front. With each passing day, they grow richer. They don't have to worry about the clock. In fact, it's their friend.[*]

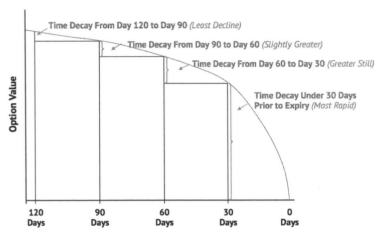

Time Remaining Until Expiration Date

Horizons' NASDAQ 100 Covered Call ETF (QYLD) takes money from covered call option buyers and pays it out as distributions to its investors. The fund simply buys the NASDAQ index and writes calls just above the current price that expire in about a month.

For a modest 0.60% management fee, you can outsource your option selling to Horizons' Covered Call ETF. The fund yielded a fat 12.9% over the past 12 months thanks to the premiums it sells to option buyers, plus the capital appreciation it enjoys from the index itself.

This sounds like a good strategy—and it is—but there are a couple of big flaws in the fund's execution:

1. It would reap larger premiums by selling covered calls

---

* Sources: https://quant.stackexchange.com/questions/2434/are-there-comprehensive-analyses-of-theta-decay-in-weekly-options
https://theoptionprophet.com/blog/the-complete-guide-on-option-theta

on individual stocks rather than the index itself, and

2. It should be selling options with even *shorter* expiration times to maximize the value that expires with each passing day.

Over time, these miscues add up. Since inception, Horizons' Covered Call has been less volatile than the NASDAQ (as you'd expect). But its investors are missing out on most of the index's upside.

Horizons' NASDAQ 100 Covered Call ETF Misses Upside

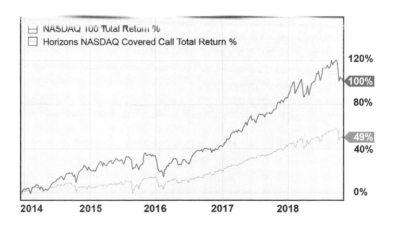

If only there were a human, not an index robot, at the helm!

Fortunately, covered call fans can upgrade to a living, breathing money manager for a modest fee. For example, Keith Hembre runs the Nuveen NASDAQ 100 Dynamic Overwrite Fund (QQQX) and employs a strategy more nuanced than Horizons. He actually buys the individual stocks and sells call options against them.

Keith usually sells options on 35% to 75% of the portfolio. He ups the percentage when Nuveen's indicators look bearish (to protect on the downside) and holds more "uncovered" positions when these stocks look bullish (to maximize upside). Keith hedges his bets.

In exchange for his expertise, we pay a management fee of 0.93%. Paying that extra 0.33% over the Horizons Covered Call ETF fee is money well spent. Keith has earned his paycheck, with his hedged gains keeping pace with the unhedged gains provided by the NASDAQ itself.

The Human Touch Matters When Selling Calls

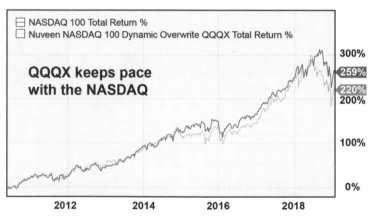

Nuveen Dynamic Overwrite pays an 8% annual yield. It sells for about its NAV today, but it has traded at a 6% discount as recently as January 2017, when it was possible to take advantage of the "free money" discount and buy the fund for just 94 cents on the dollar. And our subscribers and clients did.

We Bought the Discount, Sold the Premium

It's hard to picture now, but back then, Nuveen Dynamic Overwrite was trading at a 6% discount to NAV. That was a bigger gap than usual thanks to interest rate and general CEF and bear market worries (sound familiar?).

The headline worries remain, but Nuveen Dynamic Overwrite quickly developed quite the cachet in the income world. We received *two* dividend increases in the 15 months we owned it and enjoyed the fund's increasing popularity in the form of price gains. The fund's ticker actually rallied so much that it soon traded for a $3 *premium* to its NAV! We booked our gains when the popularity contest got out of hand and earned 42% total returns, including dividends on our investment.

Of course, past successes don't help us make money tomorrow, so let's turn our attention to the best covered call bargains today. Here are four excellent covered call funds that yield 6.6% or better, trade at discounts to their NAVs today, and have generated 7.4% returns or better since inception.

TICKER	FUND	YIELD	DISCOUNT TO NAV	RETURN ON NAV SINCE INCEPTION
ETB	Eaton Vance Buy-Write	9.1%	0.8%	7.4%
EOI	Eaton Vance Equity Income	8.0%	3.4%	6.4%
DIAX	Nuveen Dow 30 Overwrite	7.3%	2.4%	7.8%
CII	BlackRock Enhanced Capital	6.6%	5.8%	8.0%

Should we also consider cutting out the middleman and writing covered calls ourselves? It *is* possible to achieve double-digit cash payouts with a do-it-yourself strategy. We'll review a couple of examples later in this book as we discuss the best types of dividend-paying investments to write calls against. (And we can always kick a few pennies to Keith so we may kick back and let him to do it for us.)

You're probably thinking that we must be running out of high-yield investments that sidestep buying individual stocks. With 20+ investment ideas (and counting) at *Contrarian Income Report*, we've built bond portfolios using CEFs, dabbled with preferreds and convertible bonds, and even explored writing covered calls on stocks to extract more yield from America's blue-chip stocks.

If so, you're right—we're *almost* out of stock-alternative ideas. But we have *one more* important No Withdrawal concept to discuss before we "resort" to buying and holding individual stocks. We're going to use our favorite vehicle, the CEF, to buy stocks at a discount ... and get them to pay more than they ever would on their own!

Cheaper stocks with higher yields via CEFs

For those of you shaking your head at your portfolio's low yield, you can actually double or triple it *and* improve your upside potential to boot using this strategy. And it's actually *simpler* than traditional stock picking.

Many income investors have mistakenly parked their capital in "safe" consumer staples like General Mills, Kimberly-Clark, and Procter & Gamble (PG) in search of yield and security. Their money was safe, all right: their cash went nowhere—straight sideways—for the last five years!

They'd have been better off outsourcing their dividend decisions to the great Mario Gabelli. His namesake Gabelli Dividend & Income Trust Fund (GDV) tends to pay around 6% or so (6.6% today). Mario's dividends show up between the 14th and the 24th of the month, every month, to the tune of $0.11 per share. Sounds like a sweet deal, right? His investors get the benefit of a legendary money mind along with his access to ideas and cheap money. And get paid monthly too.

It really is quite the opportunity. The monthly dividends *plus* the boss's smarts have rewarded investors who made the "one-click" investing decision to buy shares in Gabelli and let Mario take care of the rest.

Super Mario: 310% Returns in 10 Years

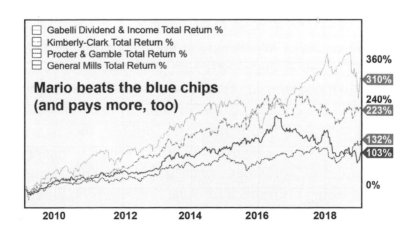

His secret sauce is his stock selection. Meanwhile *our* opportunity lies with the discount—the fact that we can wait patiently and buy it for one, to be specific. Yet, over the past three years, Gabelli Dividend & Income has traded, on average, for its NAV. No discount for Super Mario.

Today, Gabelli trades at an 8.4% discount to the value of the stocks it holds. This means we can buy these blue chips for less than 92 cents on the dollar! This deal shouldn't be available, but it is from time to time thanks to the inefficiencies in CEF-land.

The ability to snare Mario's brilliance at a bargain is one example of our "CEF edge." With $1.6 billion in assets, this particular fund is too small for big players to put money to work. Which works out perfectly for us.

Another fund with a sustainable edge is the Cohen & Steers Infrastructure Fund (UTF), which holds stock and bonds in the top infrastructure and utility companies in the world. These smart businesses own and operate utilities, airports, toll roads, railroads, and other physical framework. Now and then this CEF trades for a discount to the value of the assets it owns. The discount is generous for a fund that has returned an outstanding 9.2% per year since inception—and shows no signs of slowing down. This 9.2% return on NAV is what powers an 8.4% dividend.

Cohen & Steers Infrastructure's managers are free to travel the globe in search of a bargain. One quarter of the fund's portfolio is invested in electric utilities. The rest is a worldwide mix ranging from toll roads to airports to pipelines and more. All of these, when bought at the right price, gush growing cash, which the fund's managers both reinvest and pay to us.

Why don't we just buy these issues directly and cut out the middleman? For starters, the fund also owns positions in preferred stock shares of the infrastructure and utility companies. These pay higher yields and generally aren't available to individual investors like you and me.

Not only are we getting this collection of assets for just 94 cents on the dollar for an 8.4% annual yield with upside, but we're also putting ourselves in line for future dividend *hikes*.

Cohen & Steers Infrastructure's management team recently raised its monthly distribution *nearly 16%* (yes, you read right, from $0.134 to $0.155 per month). That's a more than generous gesture, rarely seen in the CEF world. Plus, it's not unique for this fantastic fund. This is its third big dividend increase since 2013!

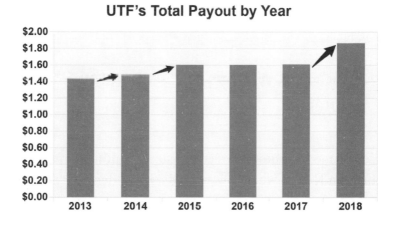

UTF's Total Payout by Year

This track record has landed the fund on our "hall of fame" list for equity CEFs. As with our previous rundowns, we rank funds by their return on NAV since inception. To qualify, the fund must pay a 5% or greater dividend and trade at a discount to its NAV. Here's the list as we went to press:

TICKER	FUND	YIELD	DISCOUNT TO NAV	RETURN ON NAV SINCE INCEPTION
HQH	Tekla Healthcare Investors	9.9%	10.0%	11.0%
UTG	Reaves Utility Income	6.6%	1.2%	10.7%
HTD	JH Tax-Advantaged Dividend Income	7.3%	4.7%	9.3%
UTF	Cohen & Steers Infrastructure	8.4%	6.3%	9.2%
RQI	Cohen & Steers Quality Income Realty	8.5%	8.8%	8.7%

Cohen & Steers Infrastructure is a most excellent fourth. But what about first, second and third? Number one Tekla Healthcare Investors (HQH) invests in the stocks of biotech and pharmaceutical firms. Its "edge" is provided by the medical doctors and researchers it hires to pick winners. And they sure do earn their money—the Tekla fund has outperformed its "dumb" ETF counterpart by a margin of 292% to 241% since inception.

The Docs Pick Winners Better than the Computers

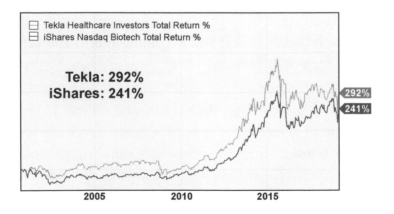

Reaves Utility Income (UTG) is a more conservative play focused on traditional utilities and telecoms. Its holdings are cash cows that will keep dishing money to investors. The fund pays 6.6% today, trades at a modest 1.2% discount to NAV, and has an excellent 15-year track record.

Big Boring Dividends Beat the Market

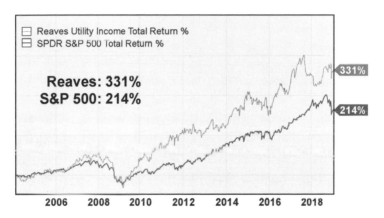

The John Hancock Tax-Advantaged Dividend Income Fund (HTD) buys a blend of common stocks and preferred shares, the latter of which are not readily available to individual investors. The firm's inside track on preferreds and smart picking of common shares has helped it handily outpace the broader market while yielding more. The fund pays a generous 7.3% today.

More Dividends *and* Better Returns

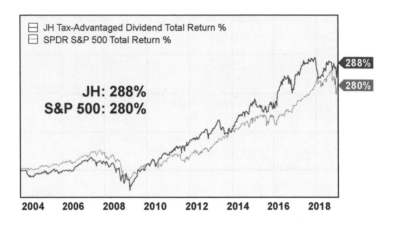

JH Tax-Advantaged Dividend Total Return %
SPDR S&P 500 Total Return %

JH: 288%
S&P 500: 280%

288%
280%

2004 2006 2008 2010 2012 2014 2016 2018

Finally, you can get the best of both REITs (real estate investment trusts, whose great benefits for income investors we'll discuss in a bit) and CEFs by picking up a closed-end fund that owns REITs, like the Cohen & Steers Quality Income Realty Fund (RQI). This fund holds some of the top REITs, including apartment landlord Essex Property Trust (ESS), cell-tower owner Crown Castle International (CCL) and data-center operator Equinix (EQIX). As you can see next, its portfolio is nicely diversified by real estate type, so you're insulated if one particular segment hits a wall:

Sector Diversification

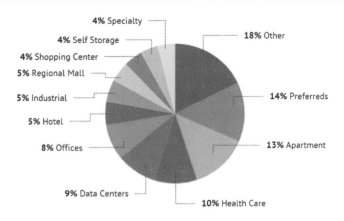

4% Specialty
4% Self Storage
4% Shopping Center
5% Regional Mall
5% Industrial
5% Hotel
8% Offices
9% Data Centers
10% Health Care
13% Apartment
14% Preferreds
18% Other

Source: Cohen & Steers September 30, 2018, fact sheet

Management firm Cohen & Steers has been around since 1986, and its team takes the outsized dividends which REITs already pay, adds in their stocks' price gains, and tops things off with a conservative amount of leverage (around 24% of the portfolio) to hand us a huge 8.5% dividend that rolls in every month like clockwork. Here's how that dividend clock ticked during a typical year:

A Predictable 8.5% Payout

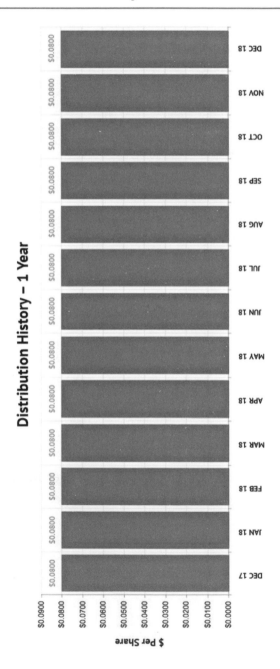

And in case you're wondering, this team knows how to spot bargains in REIT-land: check out how the Cohen & Steers Quality Income Realty Fund dominated the go-to REIT benchmark Vanguard Real Estate ETF in the last decade.

A Proven Performer

The best time to buy is right now: Cohen & Steers Quality Income Realty Fund trades at an alluring 8.8% discount to NAV. That sets us up for price upside when the fund's discount window slams shut.

In summary, there are a few reasons why stock-focused CEFs are attractive to us income hounds. As discussed at the outset of this chapter, thanks to longer life expectancies, we need our money to last us longer, which means more growth. The elite equity CEFs certainly accomplish this with total returns of 9% to 11% per year.

Secondly, they pay. We receive dividends from the CEF either monthly or quarterly. We can plan our lives around a set payout (say, 2% per quarter, which adds up to our 8% per year). Few mutual funds and ETFs offer dividends this generous.

Finally, there's that free money discount. Since CEFs have fixed pools of shares, we can be greedy and only buy them when they are in the bargain bin. The five CEFs above all trade at discounts to the values of the stocks in their portfolio today. There's no reason for a fund like Cohen & Steers Infrastructure to trade for 94 cents on the dollar, so we should take advantage of this!

So, you can build a great retirement portfolio using CEFs alone. With smart selection and purchase timing, you can collect 7% to 8% yearly dividends that are 100% powered by the fund's annual profits. Whether you choose to buy bonds, stocks, or something in between, there are excellent performers that you can purchase for 90 or 95 cents on the dollar.

However, we must point out that your *price upside* will ultimately be capped on these positions. The CEF equity all-stars above have returned 9% to 11% per year historically. This is plenty to fulfill our initial 8% No Withdrawal mandate. At these rates, our money "only" doubles every six to eight years.

What if you're looking for more? Dedicate a portion of your portfolio to grow in hopes of doubling that money every four, five, or six years? To do so, you'll need returns of at least 12% per year—which means you must add dividend *growth* to your requirements.

But the growth we highlighted from Cohen & Steers Infrastructure is rare for a CEF. We therefore look to individual stocks (covered in Chapter 8) for dividend growth. They can increase their cash flows—and then their payouts—over time. As their payouts increase, investors pay more for their stocks, which provides us with the double-digit growth potential we're looking for.

CHAPTER 7

Constructing a Safe Bond Portfolio (and More Secure High Payers to Add)

BY NOW YOU'RE starting to think about constructing a diversified dividend portfolio. Let's see how you can spread your risk and maximize your income with these six high-yield buckets.

HIGH-YIELD ASSET CLASS	AVERAGE YIELD
Commercial Landlords	7.8%
Floating-Rate Bonds	6.7%
"Go Anywhere" Bond Funds	8.0%
Infrastructure Plays	6.4%
Recession-Proof REITs	7.5%
Secure, Boring Bonds	6.5%

We've already explored floating-rate bonds, so let's now head into what we term "go anywhere" bond funds, secure boring bonds, and some bonus bond funds for those in high tax brackets. In later chapters, we'll get into the world of infrastructure plays, commercial landlords, and recession-proof REITs (real estate investment trusts).

"Go anywhere" bond funds

HIGH-YIELD ASSET CLASS	AVERAGE YIELD
Commercial Landlords	7.8%
Floating-Rate Bonds	6.7%
"Go Anywhere" Bond Funds	8.0%
Infrastructure Plays	6.4%
Recession-Proof REITs	7.5%
Secure, Boring Bonds	6.5%

You already know that we second-level thinkers have a smarter—and more profitable—way to buy bonds than combing through tens of thousands of issuances to purchase the 500 or 1,000 best ones.

Instead we cherry-pick the best managers, who in turn have access to deals that we individual investors never hear about. They get our money, and we in turn receive their expertise.

We like to buy and hold the best bond funds for many years. Good returns over time indicate "alpha"—some edge that the fund's manager has exploited year after year measured by return above a benchmark. In Bondland, inefficiencies do exist, and we want someone who can snag them for our benefit. Opportunities move from market to market, which is why you want a bond manager who can "go anywhere" to find us the best deals in fixed income. Your "go anywhere" bond funds will see their holdings change as opportunities arise. That's exactly what you want—a manager who will secure value from anywhere around the world.

The only consistency we ask for is *performance*. While returns can vary from quarter to quarter and even year to year, we demand the best managers who deliver alpha consistently over the long term. And annualized total return (distributions plus stock price) since inception is the ultimate "lifetime achievement" score. It spells out the profits a fund is generating on its portfolio over the long haul.

This chart shows the AllianceBernstein Global High-Income Fund, the same fund we used in an earlier example.

These Safe Bonds Regularly Romp Risky Stocks

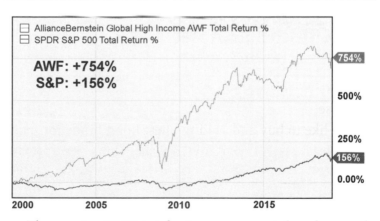

The soaring 754% total return represents bonds smartly bought by this fund's manager. Meanwhile, the "more pedestrian" 156% gain represents stocks dumbly held by the benchmark S&P 500 index. What you are seeing is that since AllianceBernstein Global High-Income's inception, there has been no contest between its bonds and the broad markets' stocks—that is, what most people own. This CEF has delivered safety, income, and upside, to the tune of 10%+ annual returns.

"They say" we investors can't have both. Dividend investors can't enjoy the income and safety of bonds and the upside of stocks. We must choose, or allocate, or whatever.

Usually "they" are academics or basic-minded advisors who haven't made their own money from the market. They live in the world of theory, while we work in the real world. And our experience is different. We have found that you don't have to choose between income now and growth later when you can achieve both with a CEF like AllianceBernstein's Global High-Income Fund. (And by the way, as we write, that fund is offering up a "free" $1.92 per share discount. How's *that* for a supposedly efficient market!)

A 14% Discount = A Free $1.92

AllianceBernstein Global High-Income heads up our top eight list of top-notch bond managers that'll work for you for free. Each of these CEFs:

- Yields more than 5%,

- Trades at a discount to NAV, and

- Has generated annualized returns of 7.5% or better since inception. (The ability to earn consistent profits is important because it shows that the dividend is sustainable over the long haul.)

TICKER	FUND	YIELD	DISCOUNT TO NAV	RETURN ON NAV SINCE INCEPTION
AWF	AllianceBernstein Global High-Income	7.6%	13.8%	10.5%
BBN	BlackRock Taxable Muni Bond	6.5%	2.5%	9.2%
CHI	Calamos Convertible Opps	9.6%	2.2%	9.1%
HYT	BlackRock Corporate High Yield	8.8%	12.8%	8.0%
LDP	Cohen & Steers Limited Duration	8.2%	4.4%	7.9%
FFC	Flaherty & Crumrine Preferreds	7.5%	2.1%	7.7%
BIT	BlackRock Multi-Sector Income	8.8%	13.2%	7.7%
HIX	Western Asset High Income	8.9%	12.7%	7.6%

If you're looking for tax exempt bonds, you may be attracted to the BlackRock Taxable Muni Bond Fund (BBN) at number two, with its juicy 6.5% yield and 9.2% annualized return since inception. However, that yield is only partly tax exempt, because the fund also buys taxable bonds. There are other municipal bond funds that focus exclusively on tax exempt bonds, so let's explore these tax deals in more detail and highlight our favorite funds to buy.

Municipal bonds

HIGH-YIELD ASSET CLASS	AVERAGE YIELD
Commercial Landlords	7.8%
Floating-Rate Bonds	6.7%
"Go Anywhere" Bond Funds	8.0%
Infrastructure Plays	6.4%
Recession-Proof REITs	7.5%
Secure, Boring Bonds	6.5%

Municipal ("muni") bonds can provide you with 5%+ distributions that Uncle Sam won't touch. Plus, income investors buying smartly today pay as little as 88 cents on the dollar!

Municipal bonds are bonds issued by states, cities, and counties to raise money—often for capital projects like public transportation and infrastructure improvements. Interest paid by munis is often tax exempt at the federal as well as the state level, which makes them favorites of folks in high tax brackets. For example, if you live in California, you can stash some California munis in your portfolio and pay no federal or state taxes on the interest you earn.

It all sounds like a great deal for the investor—and it usually is. The only thing that can go wrong is when your city (Detroit in 2013) or county (Orange County in 1994) or state (the "51st state," Puerto Rico, right now) defaults on its debt obligations, in which case you may only get a few dimes for your investment dollar (though Detroit bondholders received up to 74 cents—still not good).

These default events are extremely rare given the total number of municipalities in the US. But when they do happen, they're spectacular enough disasters that they scare most investors away for several months. This usually creates an outstanding buying opportunity.

For quick profits, it's actually best to buy munis after mini-panics. These seem to happen every year or two, presenting us level-headed contrarians with safe yields for cheap. Anyone who followed this advice and bought munis after the irrational "tax plan panic" in November 2016, when fear gripped the markets that the Trump tax plan would lower tax rates and "no one would want munis," enjoyed total returns of up to 16.7% in just 12 months!

Muni Selloffs Set the Stage for Quick Profits

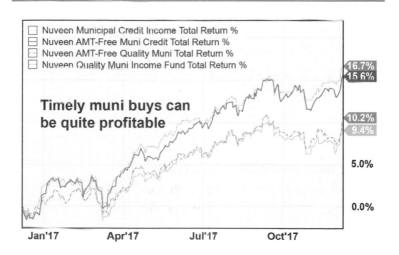

For investors looking for steady monthly paychecks, the best time to buy munis is usually anytime—*especially* for those in a high tax bracket. Muni distributions, after all, typically get a pass from Uncle Sam at the federal level. (And state-specific funds will extend that dividend courtesy to your state's tax return as well.)

Headline-reading investors fret about things like "spreads" in munis—or their interest rate advantage over US Treasuries. The margin is as thin as it's been in years. And it's a valid concern for those who *don't* know how to buy the right muni bonds. But investors who *do* know munis are banking 5%+ tax-free yields today. And some are even securing big margins of safety too! How? Simply by selecting the best muni CEFs.

Buying a CEF is even easier than buying individual muni bonds. We simply enter the ticker in an online brokerage account, click the "Buy" button and we've got a fund with a handpicked portfolio of 900+ muni bonds (and monthly distributions).

Our tax-free distributions get even better when we buy at a discount to NAV. An 8% discount, for example, means we're buying $1 worth of munis for just $0.92.

It *also* means that we receive *more yield*. For example, Nuveen's AMT-Free Municipal Credit Income Fund pays a 5.1% distribution on its NAV. But investors who buy shares today at an 8% discount will actually earn 5.5% on their investment.

Plus, there's more:

1. The 5.5% yield is exempt from federal taxes, and

2. The fund's 8% discount is potential upside for us if and when this window closes.

Not interested in selling? That's fine. Buy these funds at a discount anyway to protect your downside risk.

Here are five muni funds that are bargains today. All five pay 5% or more, are exempt from federal taxes, *and* trade for a 6% to 12% discount to the value of their underlying bond portfolios.

These funds have also been excellent long-term investments. This is important because, in our experience, past performance is the best indicator of future results in CEF-land. This is especially the case for munis, where the best managers consistently deliver alpha thanks to their "unfair" advantages (connections and capital) in this less-than-efficient corner of the market.

5 Muni Funds with 5%+ Tax-Free Yields

TICKER	FUND	YIELD	DISCOUNT TO NAV	RETURN ON NAV SINCE INCEPTION
VMO	Invesco Muni Opps	5.7%	8.7%	6.1%
NZF	Nuveen Muni Credit Income	5.6%	7.7%	6.1%
NMZ	Nuveen Muni High Income	5.5%	5.4%	6.1%
BFK	BlackRock Muni Income	5.5%	6.6%	5.9%
NVG	Nuveen AMT-Free Muni Credit	5.5%	8.2%	6.0%

Each of these funds has returned 6% or better on its portfolio since inception, which means that the managers are well connected and know what they're doing. They are also poised to outperform their historical norms, thanks to the generous discounts they trade at today.

We now move on toward the world of stocks. As with bonds, we have better strategies than simply "buying" them and "hoping" they'll go up in price. Let's talk about some lesser-known "hybrid" vehicles that will pay us more in yield, with less risk, than stocks-at-large.

CHAPTER 8

Stocks

MOST DIVIDEND INVESTORS understandably love the idea of an 8% No Withdrawal Portfolio. It's a simple yet "game-changing" idea that you don't hear much from mainstream pundits and advisors: *Find stocks that pay 6%, 7%, 8%, or more and you can retire comfortably, living off dividend checks while your initial capital stays intact (or even appreciates).*

But it's not a simple as screening for 8% yields and buying them. We must smartly select the stocks that are going to pay our dividends securely—*without tapping their own share prices to pay us.*

> When a stock pays a dividend, its share price is reduced by that amount. We don't want the stock price to decline over time below the value of dividends paid out. That's "tapping the stock price," which means we aren't receiving the full dividend yield when we sell.

Today, there are 123 stocks with market caps above $500 million trading on major US exchanges and that yield 8% or more. A basket of these dividends is going to be a mixed bag, however. While some of these stocks will shower you with quarterly (or even monthly) payouts with price appreciation to boot, others will *lose* some or all of your cash in price depreciation (the price drops).

Of our 123 candidates, *99 have not delivered 40% total returns over the past five years.* And this is the minimum we ask of an 8% payer—dish us our dividend and don't lose our initial capital!

Granted, this back of the envelope study is probably a bit harsh. We're missing a few elite 8% payers that "graduated" to lower yields thanks to good stock performances. Still, the important lesson here is that 8% payout success is challenging (though not impossible, as we'll see shortly).

Of these 99 high-paying underperformers, we have 57 "biggest losers." These stocks have actually *lost* their investors' money over the past five years. In other words, they have delivered their big dividends yet lost as much (or more) in price, while the S&P 500 gained 61%. Not good!

So while we can expect that our steadier strategy may underperform during roaring bull markets, we would expect a business to *at least beat your mattress* as a total return vehicle.

Exceptions? Sure. Business models can change, and past performance isn't necessarily a predictor of future results. For example, New Residential Investment (NRZ), a REIT, declined in price three years ago. It had a completely different portfolio then than it does now. Here's why and how it matters.

Mortgage REITs (mREITs) like New Residential typically buy mortgage loans from lenders and collect the interest. Their business model prints money when long-term rates are steady or, better yet, declining. When long-term rates drop, these existing mortgages become more valuable (because new loans pay less).

On the other hand, the mREIT gravy train usually derails when rates rise and these mortgage portfolios *decline* in value. Historically, rising-rate environments have been very bad for mREITs and have resulted in deadly dividend cuts.

New Residential bucked rising rates and actually doubled its investors' money and the value of its own portfolio (its book value) in less than three years. Its secret? Rather than buying mortgages, the firm has been investing in mortgage service rights (MSRs). This is "the right" to collect payments from a borrower. In other words, New Residential doesn't own these loans—it owns the rights to service these loans.

MSRs tend to rise in value when mortgage refinancing slows down. That's exactly what happened, and this "pivot" has made many retirement riches. Happy investors have collected double-digit dividends while enjoying price appreciation to the tune of 151% total returns!

An Ideal 11.8% Dividend Payer

New Residential's success story is rarer than not in 8%-ville. But these winners *are* around, and we'll uncover them in a minute. First, let me call out a loser that, despite its high current yield, doesn't really belong in a retirement portfolio. Fashion retailer Buckle Inc (BKE) pays 5.6%, but the dividend well might run dry soon.

Buckle's sales have been in a slow-motion nosedive for three years, taking earnings and free cash flow down with them.

Belt Tightens on Buckle's Payout

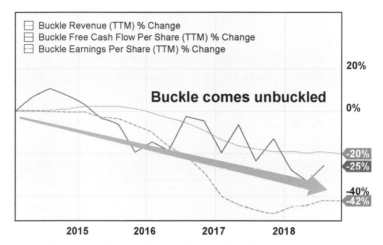

Why are sales suffering? The firm's revenues are drying up with its flailing retail outlets. Buckle must pivot its business model to sell direct to consumers *online* in order to survive.

These "death of retail" market stresses (due to Amazon), predictably, have driven up Buckle's payout ratios: in the last 12 months, the company paid out more than it earned in dividends (139% of profits, to be precise), along with 135% of free cash flow. Any way you slice it, the company is taking on debt to fund its dividend. It simply doesn't have the cash flow to afford its current shareholder payment. It's borrowing from Peter to pay Paul.

We don't like to see payout ratios above 50% from non-REITs, let alone 100%. This dividend has too high a risk of becoming unbuckled to belong in a No Withdrawal Portfolio.

CenturyLink (CTL) is a recent example of a high-yield

trap. The telecom company paid dividends and yielded a whopping 14.4%, but we warned that investors shouldn't compare it to AT&T (T) or Verizon (VZ) because its payout was much more precarious.

CenturyLink is one of a number of regional communications companies that simply didn't have the scale to compete with the likes of AT&T and Verizon but have piled up a mountain of debt trying to. After a few acquisitions in the late '00s and early '10s, CenturyLink finally cried "uncle" in 2013 and slashed its dividend by roughly a quarter, from 72.5 cents to 54 cents.

CenturyLink's high dividend in early 2019 was simply the result of battered shares that have plunged almost 45% in the past five years or so. The top line eroded, profits stagnated, and the dividends ate up an ever-larger chunk of its cash. This cramped the company's financial flexibility and left it mostly unable to continue acquiring its way to scale.

CenturyLink's payout cut didn't help its payout *ratio*, which remained an extremely dangerous 129%. And how *was* the company funding its payment to shareholders, you ask? With skyrocketing debt, of course!

A Dangerous Dividend Combo: High Payout Ratio Plus Debt

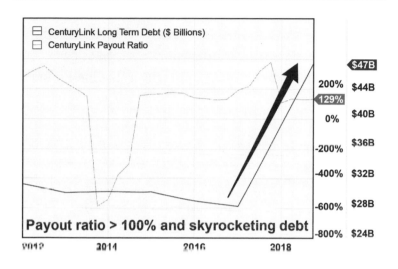

Debt and nosebleed payout ratio were indeed fatal flaws for this dividend. CEO Jeffrey Storey insisted the dividend was safe, but what else was the guy going to say? On February 13, 2019, lack of cash forced CenturyLink's board's hand and they chopped their stock's payout in half. Again.

The name L Brands (LB) probably won't spark much in your memory banks, but its brands certainly will—Victoria's Secret and Bath & Body Works, as well as Pink, La Senza, and Henri Bendel.

Victoria's Secret and Bath & Body Works, specifically, are practically royalty among mall-store names—but that's a tarnished throne on which to sit. And L Brands' operations and stock-price performance both reflect that. The company's dividend yields 6.3%. But the lingerie peddler's payout is on borrowed time—and when it goes, it's going to catch the first-level types completely off guard, pummeling the stock again.

That's because all those folks following the net income–based payout have no idea! Sure, L Brands pays out 87% of its paper profits as dividends. That's quite high, though not necessarily a sign of a looming cut on its own.

However, its cash payout ratio tells a *far* different story.

Key Indicator Flips from Yellow to Red

Over the last few months, the company has gone from paying a high-but-manageable portion of FCF (free cash flow, the cash left after a company pays expenses and invests in property, plant and equipment) as dividends to paying out *more* in dividends than it earns in FCF. *It's a subtle shift that most dividend investors sleepwalk right by.* This ticking timebomb has no place in a secure No Withdrawal Portfolio.

Dividend growth for 12%+ annual returns

Dividend raises, sooner or later, are reflected in a price increase for the stock. They are the surest way to ensure price upside in addition to our current yield.

For example, take a stock that pays a 3% current yield and then hikes its payout by 10%. It's unlikely that its stock price will stagnate for long. Investors will see the new 3.3% yield, higher than it's been and likely higher than its long-term average, and buy more shares. They'll drive the price up and the yield back down—eventually towards 3%. This is why your favorite dividend "aristocrat," a company everyone knows and has paid dividends forever, *never* pays a high current yield—its stock price rises too fast!

Let's revisit Johnson & Johnson, which always seems to pay between 2% and 3% or so. Its current 2.8% yield already gets you ahead of the game in today's low-rate world. Next, consider the stock's price appreciation, which moves remarkably in tandem with its dividend. Sometimes it drifts higher, sometimes lower, but it always finds its way back to match its stair-stepping payout.

J&J's Payout Drives Stock Price Growth

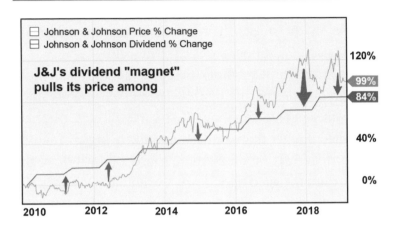

Johnson and Johnson's 2.8% yield disqualifies the stock from consideration for our No Withdrawal Portfolio. When we buy the stock, it requires too much "hope" that we will reach our income goals. So let's dust off our previous example, hospital landlord Medical Properties Trust.

Medical Properties raises its dividend like clockwork every year by about 5%. Add these raises to its 5.9% yield, and we have a formula for 10.9% total returns per year because the stock price over time follows the dividend hikes:

Medical Properties' Yield Today	5.9%
Yearly Dividend Growth	+5.0%
Total Returns Per Year	=10.9%

Medical Properties' dividend acts like a "magnet" for its share price. The stock may stray for days, weeks, or months, but eventually it finds its way back to its payout.

Price Rises with Its Payout

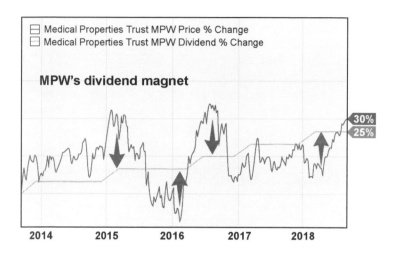

The consistently rising dividend provides a natural lift to the share price over time. So, we can focus our purchases on share prices that are "lagging behind" their dividends. This is similar to our strategy of buying CEFs at discounts to their NAVs—we are using the same approach here, with the dividend stream acting as the value anchor.

Take any stock and map out its stock price versus its dividend over a multiyear period and you'll be amazed at how closely they track each other. It's no accident. Rising dividends create rising stock prices because they create more valuable underlying assets. Here's another example— blue-chip healthcare landlord Ventas (VTR). The firm has steadily raised its dividend this decade, and its stock price has climbed along with it:

Ventas Raises Dividend, Which Raises Stock Price

This happens because Ventas, give or take a point, tends to pay a 5% *current* yield.

At Any Moment, Ventas Probably Pays About 5%

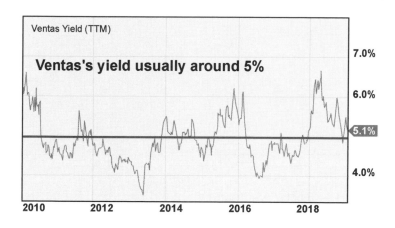

Which means as Ventas raises its dividend, investors are willing to pay more for its now-higher payout. So, the price rises in tandem. If you raise the water in a tub (increase the dividend yield), a rubber duck (stock price) rises with it, bringing the yield back to its long-term average.

Let's map out the case of Ventas with some round numbers to make the math easy. We'll say the stock is a 5% payer growing its dividend by 5% per year. Its current yield (left column) stays constant amidst the dividend growth because its stock price (right column) rises along with its dividend.

YIELD	YEAR	DIVIDEND (5%/year)	STOCK PRICE
5%	4	$1.22	$24.40
5%	3	$1.16	$23.20
5%	2	$1.105	$22.10
5%	1	$1.0525	$21.05
5%	0	$1.00	$20.00

This is exactly what happened with Medical Properties. It has a "yield ceiling" because when investors see its dividend looking particularly juicy, they buy the stock.

MPW's "Yield Ceiling" Is High at 8% or 9%

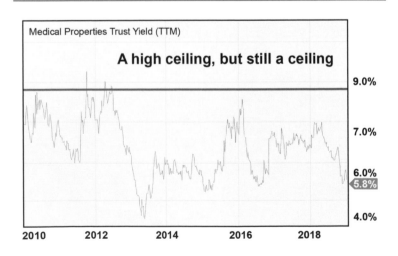

Here's the same chart above with the stock price overlaid. Notice that *peaks in yield tend to correspond with*

buying opportunities in Medical Properties shares. This means when yields spike, not only do you get more dividend for your dollar, but you also get more price upside too!

Buy the High Yields for Big Price Upside

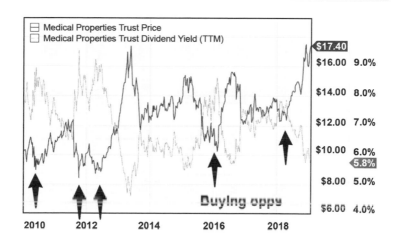

We'll talk about stock timing later in this chapter. First, let's focus on which stocks to buy to maximize our dividends per dollar and our price upside!

As you can probably infer, dividend growth is the key. And if we had decades to build our wealth, we could assemble a portfolio of high-quality dividend growers and let them compound us to riches. But we income-focused investors have a greater sense of urgency. We need yield today in addition to upside tomorrow. There's a reason we chose Medical Properties over, for example, Apple. So, let's focus our attention on dividend growers who already pay 6% or better. In doing so, we'll discuss two asset buckets filled with companies that receive favored tax treatment from Uncle Sam.

REITs for yields today and growth tomorrow

REITs carry a wee bit more drama than our fixed-income funds, at least in their stock prices. But even that's positive for us, as you'll see. It's where opportunity lies. Their dividends are paid consistently every quarter. And they trend higher over time, pulling the stock price up too. Unlike CEFs, which have modest capital appreciation potential, REITs have wonderful "built-in" capital appreciation potential.

HIGH-YIELD ASSET CLASS	AVERAGE YIELD
Commercial Landlords	7.8%
Floating-Rate Bonds	6.7%
"Go Anywhere" Bond Funds	8.0%
Infrastructure Plays	6.4%
Recession-Proof REITs	7.5%
Secure, Boring Bonds	6.5%

REITs, as the name suggests, typically own or finance real estate. On the finance side, we also have "mREITs," such as New Residential, which buy up residential mortgages, and "commercial mREITs," such as Ladder Capital (LADR) and Blackstone Mortgage Trust (BXMT), which lend money for commercial properties.

The special arrangement REITs have with the IRS

REITs pay big dividends *and* outperform stocks at

large (more on this in a minute) because of their special tax status. The Internal Revenue Service lets REITs avoid paying income taxes if they pay out most of their earnings to shareholders. To be precise, they must pay out 90% or more of their income as dividends. In return, REITs can deduct these dividends from their income tax bill, which means they effectively *pay little or no corporate taxes.* Which means they can pay out more to investors!

To qualify, the IRS requires that 75% of REIT profits come from real estate. As a result, these firms tend to collect rent checks, pay their bills, and send most of the rest of the cash to us as dividends.

And our smart No Withdrawal strategy of buying REITs is finally being confirmed by the Wall Street wonks. A recent study, "Historical Returns of the Market Portfolio,"[*] examined asset classes worldwide from all the way back to 1960 through 2015. Its conclusion? *REITs are the best investments you can buy.*

During that 55-year period, REITs delivered 6.4% yearly returns *after* inflation. They beat stocks (5.5%), non-government bonds (3.5%), and government bonds alike (3.1%). Check out the chart below, which shows REITs (labeled "real estate") steadily beating the rest of the field.

---

[*]   https://papers.ssrn.com/sol3/papers.cfm?abstract_id=2978509

Study Shows REITs Outperform over Decades

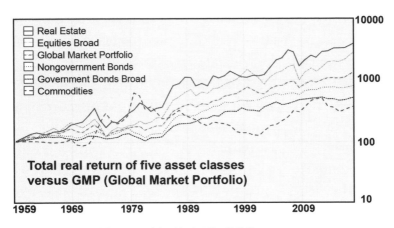

Source: "Historical Returns of the Market Portfolio"

The sector's most popular fund is the Vanguard Real Estate ETF. It pays a respectable 4.4% today and outperformed the S&P 500 from inception until things changed in 2018.

Vanguard REIT ETF versus the S&P 500

We can "fix" Vanguard Real Estate's recent underperformance by avoiding its troubled holdings (such as retail REITs) and focusing on more recession-proof properties (such as healthcare facilities). We'll discuss the most desirable real estate sectors for REITs today in a moment.

Sector selection is important because we need robust occupancy and cash flows to drive future dividend growth. The best REITs to buy are those that raise their payouts regularly. As we've previously stressed, returns from dividend stocks come from current yield *plus* their future dividend growth rates, and REITs are no different.

> **Returns from dividend stocks come from current yield *plus* their future dividend growth rates.**

For a stock or REIT, dividend growth is the big driver of price appreciation. When a firm increases its payout, boosting the stock's yield, its current yield doesn't stay higher for long. Investors flock to the stock because of its bigger dividend, bringing its price up and its yield back towards previous levels.

Let's look at the 10 (and only 10) REITs paying 7% or more that have generously raised their payouts over the last three years. Pay special attention to the "total return" column on the far right. Their combination of generous current yields and payout hikes has generally pleased their investors.

TICKER	STOCK	YIELD	3-YEAR DIVIDEND GROWTH	3-YEAR TOTAL RETURNS
GNL	Global Net Lease	10.6%	59.3%	28.7%
CLNY	Colony Capital	8.1%	58.0%	0.9%
ARI	Apollo Commercial Real Estate	10.4%	42.9%	54.4%
BXMT	Blackstone Mortgage Trust	7.4%	40.8%	74.4%
NRZ	New Residential Investment	12.2%	35.8%	125.1%
SBRA	Sabra Health Care REIT	9.2%	30.7%	26.5%
OHI	Omega Healthcare Investors	6.8%	26.7%	43.1%
KRG	Kite Realty Group Trust	8.2%	22.4%	-26.2%
BRX	Brixmor Property Group	6.8%	22.4%	-25.9%
TWO	Two Harbors Investment	13.1%	15.2%	71.8%

While past returns may be no guarantee of future results, past dividend hikes tend to be a very good indicator of future raises. (Think of our experience with the best CEFs, where the same managers beat the field year after year.) So, let's project future dividend growth while we focus on the sectors with the best business fundamentals.

Following the money for dividend growth

First, let's follow the money. Funds from operations (FFO) represent the amount of cash a REIT actually generates. It's where our dividend originates, which makes it the building block for everything else in the REIT world.

To calculate FFO, we start with net income. Then we add back depreciation and amortization (which are accounting expenses) and subtract profits from property sales (which are one-time events).

REITs are required to pay most of their earnings back to shareholders as dividends—but those are just *paper* profits. FFO represents the *actual rent checks* that can be shoveled back to us as cash dividends.

Obviously, we want to see FFO per share in excess of the dividend per share. If it's not, it means the dividend isn't really "covered" and management is funding the payout with borrowed money. Potential danger ahead.

We generally look for dividend-to-FFO payout ratios below 80% for REITs. Again, every firm is different, and some can get away with a higher percentage than others. Pay attention to management: most competent teams will say what their target ratio is. Note this and hold them to it.

Declining ratios are often a good sign because they indicate rising FFO. They're often a precursor to dividend increases. What drives FFO higher? Rising demand for the company's properties, of course. Higher occupancies mean higher rent checks—and bigger dividends for you.

We do not recommend you run out and buy the Vanguard Real Estate ETF. To start, even though its 4.4% payout looks appealing, it's only a bit more than half of what we'd need to fuel our 8% yield—and keep our No Withdrawal strategy chugging along.

Second, as we discussed earlier, it contains a broad basket of real estate firms for better and for worse. For example, nearly 15% of its portfolio is real estate landlords. Their rent checks are sitting right in the way of Jeff Bezos and Amazon (AMZN). The humongous internet retailer is eating alive brick-and-mortar competitors like Macy's (M), L Brands, Buckle, and Guess (GES). These chains appear to be in permanent trouble, which is a big problem for their landlords (and *their* REIT investors).

We wouldn't want to bet a penny of our retirement cash against Amazon retail "disrupter-in-chief" Jeff Bezos. The equivalent of the investing phrase "Don't fight the Fed" in today's REIT-world is "Don't fight Amazon."

Instead, we're going to suggest that you focus on REITs that are already raising their rents without any problem. Their higher and higher cash flows will help assure you're not settling for the "mere" 8% *total returns* that their generous current yields would suggest. You should reap stock price gains on top of high dividends too.

The best industries for REITs today

Today there are three REIT sectors that don't fight Amazon or any internet trends:

1. Healthcare

Healthcare landlords are riding a demographic bull market, with 10,000 baby boomers hitting 65 every day. Demand for places like skilled nursing facilities (SNFs) and hospitals continues to rise. Total patient days at SNFs are not only *increasing* but are projected to accelerate higher in the coming years.

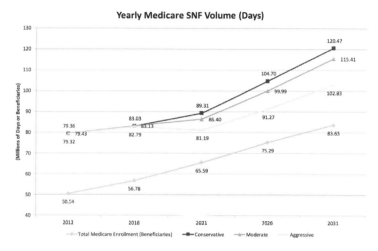

(Source: Avalere Health, a leading healthcare consultancy)

2. Industrial Warehouses

This asset class is growing just as fast as Amazon. Yet it's much cheaper, *and*—if you buy right—you can bank a soaring stream of dividends as well.

First-level investors—the basic types who buy and sell off headlines without deeper thought—believe that they must purchase Amazon itself to profit from the e-commerce boom. We instead consider what Amazon CEO Jeff Bezos (and other e-commerce entrepreneurs) will need to gobble up to keep their firms growing. By purchasing ahead of them, we can then "lease" our asset back to them (at higher and higher rates, of course).

This asset is warehouses, which are becoming the hottest industrial property in America.

This trend has been gaining steam since the internet went mainstream. Warehouse demand has enjoyed a nonstop boom thanks to online shopping.

US E-Commerce Sales (in Millions)

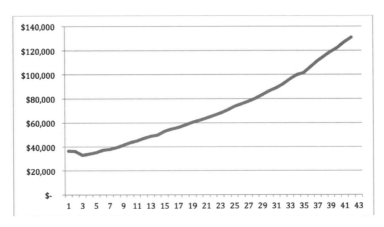

(Source: US Census Bureau)

Think about the number of deliveries you receive every week. Each package starts in a warehouse somewhere. *The Economist* reports that online sellers (including Amazon) will need 2.3 billion square feet of new warehousing over the next 20 years* to fulfill their increasing order volume. And these firms want their warehouses to be close to big cities (where most of the online orders must be shipped to).

3. Commercial landlords

Commercial loans are more complex than residential loans—which is a good thing for skilled lenders (and their investors). A firm with a bit of subject matter expertise can really set itself apart from the pretenders. And the need for commercial financing is booming. Loans are up tenfold in the last eight years, yet banks are leaving the business!

---

*   https://www.economist.com/special-report/2017/10/28/the-future-of-online-retailing-is-bright

Recent regulations like the international Basel III rule, agreed upon in 2010, more than doubled the capital requirements for banks (from 2% to 4.5% of common equity). It means they need more cash on hand for every dollar they lend out. Good for reducing bank runs, but bad for lending—and bank profits.

Most banks don't want to deal with the headaches, so they've already stepped away from the commercial market. As they flee, boutique commercial lenders step in to write mortgages for commercial properties. It's a lucrative, robust market ripe for REITs today.

By smartly selecting your REIT sectors, you can diversify your portfolio so that, if demand softens in one sector, the others can pick up the slack. You can also find some REITs that offer diversification within their portfolios, but it's important to diversify your REIT holdings among a few managers too.

When to buy REITs #1: When there are headline worries for all REITs

As we highlighted earlier with Medical Properties, we periodically have the opportunity to buy a REIT when its yield is high and its price is low. Typically we can thank:

- Headline worries about the sector (for example, that rising rates always hurt REITs), and/or

- Company-specific worries.

Let's start with big-picture concerns, which weighed on REIT stock prices at various times in 2016, 2017, and

2018. The culprit was the Fed, which began and continued to raise rates.

Conventional wisdom about REITs, as with bonds, says they will perform poorly in a rising-rate environment. It sounds reasonable enough. Rising rates increase REIT borrowing costs, squeezing profits and potentially narrowing payouts. There is also the more superficial explanation that REITs, because they are viewed as primarily income producing by those who don't understand the stock price gain potential, act like bonds—rates up, prices down.

Over the short term, there may indeed be many days when a lower Treasury price and higher yield will send REIT prices lower.

A Short-Run Seesaw between REITs and T-Bill Yields

But that's a lazy blanket statement that just hasn't been

the case historically over any meaningful period. As REIT investors, *we care about years, not days.*

Let's rewind again to June 2004 to June 2006, when the federal funds rate rose from 1% to 5.25% while the 10-year Treasury glided higher from 4.5% to 5.15%. Those are serious increases that can affect business borrowing costs and investor profits substantially.

So, you'd think it was a terrible time for REITs, right? *Wrong—and really wrong.* The Vanguard Real Estate ETF returned an extraordinary 48.1% including dividends over this period, crushing the S&P 500's 14.6% gain.

REITs Crushed Other Stocks as Rates Rose …

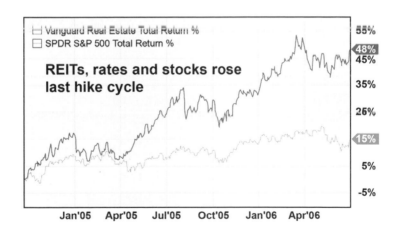

Let's fast-forward to *this* rate hike cycle,* and we see

---

*   The Fed appeared to be in a rising rate mood through December 2018. It's impossible to determine where rates will go at any particular time (or everyone would be making money predicting interest rates, which they are not, but many people make money talking about them), but there will be rising and falling rate environments. It's important to understand that carefully selected REITs have performed well in both rising and declining rate environments.

that the REIT bears are patting themselves on the back. After all, the sector at large has indeed underperformed the broader market since the Fed started moving again in December 2015.

REITs Lag—If You Believe the Flawed Vanguard Real Estate ETF

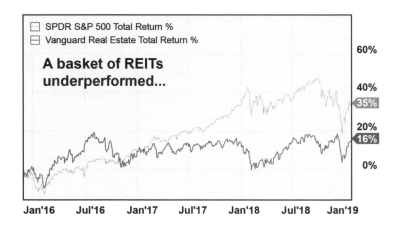

However, when we filter for better quality than we get from this passive index, we see that the best REITs have had no problem with the current Fed either. Excellent healthcare landlords like Ventas, Medical Properties, and Omega Healthcare have all outpaced the market this rate hike cycle. And Medical Properties more than doubled the S&P 500's return!

Smart REIT Investors Had No Rate Problem, However

Due to the urban legend that higher interest rates are bad for REITs, headlines continue to whipsaw REIT share prices in the short term. Plus, every 90 days, REITs report their earnings to Wall Street (and file with the SEC), which opens the door for something to be misinterpreted or miscommunicated. But the short-term "bad news" often results in great long-term buying opportunities for us. In fact, to find a REIT paying 8% or more usually requires some type of "negative price catalyst"—a headline that spooks investors, dropkicks the price, and increases the yield. So, if you want to invest in REITs, watch out for bad headlines and run towards them for what could be a very profitable opportunity. *Especially* if we focus on the REITs that are growing their payouts consistently.

First-level investors fret that when rates rise, REITs will suffer. They view REITs as mere "bond proxies" that lose their attractiveness when fixed-income investments pay more. But they're missing the power of dividend growth, which illustrates that the best defense is a good offense. Let's start with research from Nuveen showing that dividend growth stocks outperform everything else in the 36 months after a Fed rate increase.

Performance after the Fed Increases Rates

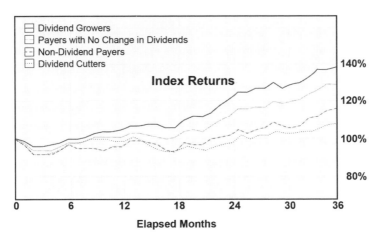

Source: Ned Davis Research

And how about a historical example from the last rate hike? Let's review the three-year period starting in May 2003 when the 10-year US Treasury yield climbed a full 200 basis points—from 3.2% to 5.2%. (We don't think rates will actually get that high this cycle, but let's consider the possibility anyway.)

REIT dividend growers like Omega Healthcare and Ventas climbed higher right alongside long-term rates. Their secret? Their rising dividends simply outran higher interest rates. (Note: We exclude Medical Properties here because it did not become a publicly traded company until 2005.)

Dividend Growth Drives Big Returns (July 2003–July 2006)

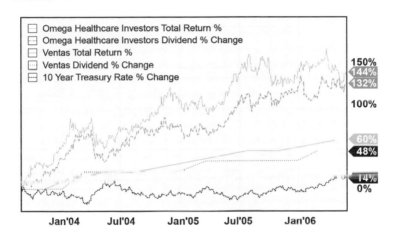

STOCK	DIVIDEND GROWTH	TOTAL RETURN
Omega Healthcare (OHI)	60%	144%
Ventas (VTR)	41%	132%

Unsurprisingly, Omega Healthcare and Ventas have been excellent performers *this* rate hike cycle too. Their investors are up 44% and 37%, respectively, since the Fed kicked into action in December 2015.

It wasn't always smooth sailing for Omega Healthcare this cycle. Amidst broader sector concerns, there were company-specific worries on and off over the past several years.

When to buy REITs #2: When there are (unfair) company-specific worries

The year 2018 started inauspiciously for Omega Health-care when the REIT announced a dividend "freeze." The stock slipped. But a freeze isn't the same as a cut—and Omega Healthcare's payout was well covered by its FFO.

The misunderstanding would soon be our clients' and subscribers' gain, as the stock yielded 10% (thanks to years of previous dividend hikes). And anytime that Omega Healthcare has paid double digits in the past, it marked a major bottom for the stock. So why would this time be any different? As you can see here, the company's generous yield limited its stock's downside.

OHI's a Screaming Buy When It Pays 10% (or Close to It)

Let's "zoom in" to see how Omega Healthcare per-formed off its latest buy signal. On April 20, 2018, the stock paid a sky-high 10.2% as investors fretted about problem operators in Omega's portfolio. Some of its skilled nursing facility operators (SNF) were having financial problems of their own and were late in paying their bills.

We analyzed the situation and realized that the prob-lem was operator specific rather than Omega specific (and, fortunately, decided to keep the stock in our recommended portfolios). In other words, the company simply had to replace the deadbeat operators and its cash flow would be humming again. That's exactly what happened, and Omega rallied to return 64% including dividends while the broader market traded sideways!

OHI's Latest Buy Signal Delivered Fast 64% Returns

(Another reason for our confidence was Omega's excellent leadership team. CEO Taylor Pickett has been at the helm for a fantastic 18 years in which he's delivered 3,000%+ total returns to investors.)

Secure REIT yields like Omega's are the truly the "rubber duckies" of the investing world. Mr. Market can push them underwater for a period of time, but eventually, they rocket up to the surface.

Let's watch this in action *again* for fun and profit. We often get questions about "2008," so let's rewind 11 years to the top of the last extended bull market. If you were savvy enough to time the top in 2007, you would still have been doing yourself a disservice by selling your shares (not least, how you would know when to have "gotten back in"?)! This dividend payer barely went below water.

Omega Healthcare: A Rare Great Performer in 2008

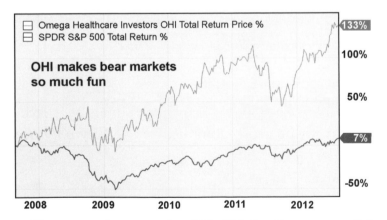

Five years later, as the S&P 500 finally recovered its crash losses, Omega investors had already enjoyed 133% returns, including steady, fat payouts throughout. And while the presence of a dividend does not *guarantee* protection from losses, examples like this one show that payout-focused investors have a serious edge in the markets.

Here's why. A falling price attracts more dividend buyers. Let's take a $20 stock with a $1 dividend (a 5% yield) that begins dropping in price. As it declines, income investors buy it because they are now able to secure *more* dividend for their initial dollar.

> **Buying REIT stocks for their dividends alone makes day-to-day price action irrelevant.**

STOCK PRICE	DIVIDEND	YIELD
$20		5%
$16.67		6%
$14.29	$1.00	7%
$12.50		8%
$10		10%

Which means that REIT investors need not concern themselves with short-term price action. *They only need to consider if the underlying payout is safe.*

Again, when selecting REITs, know that one of the key criteria is to look for those that raise their dividends regularly. Remember, returns from dividend stocks come from their current yield *plus* their future dividend growth rate, and REITs are no different. Investors will bid up the stock price as the payout increases, which keeps the yield relatively constant over time and brings profits from price gains.

No matter the interest rate environment, income investors want to own stocks that consistently increase their dividends by meaningful amounts. Here's another example using our friends at Medical Properties. It wasn't always smooth sailing here either.

Medical Properties is the only publicly traded company that invests solely in hospitals. The company was founded in 2003 by three industry veterans, led by chairman, president, and CEO Ed Aldag, who admitted they had "zero assets, a dream, and a business plan."

Years ago, hospitals didn't have mortgage financing available to them. And traditional corporate loan packages would force hospitals to lock up all of their asset value as collateral. So Ed's team set out to offer lease financing as a low-cost and flexible alternative. Thus far, it's been a fantastic niche—Ed & Co. have grown their zero assets to a $6.4 billion market cap company!

Ed is still chairman, president, and CEO of Medical Properties, pursuing his vision as only an owner–manager can. His business plan has evolved into an effective model that is increasingly showering shareholders with cash. So shouldn't we "bet on Ed" and buy any pullback in his firm's stock price?

As a second-level thinker, you would have questioned the drop in share price towards the end of 2016, which indeed offered a nice time to buy. Reading through the company's reports and looking at the bigger picture, you would have discovered that nervous investors dumped

Medical Properties for two reasons: a problem client and interest rate concerns (of course).

Let's start with the problem client. Adeptus Health (ADPT) operates freestanding emergency rooms in Texas and Colorado. It represented 6% of Medical Properties' 2017 revenues. On November 2, 2016, Adeptus surprised Wall Street with a disastrous third-quarter earnings report. It missed estimates, slashed full-year guidance, and admitted it had only $6.1 million left in the bank. Its stock crashed—and it took landlord Medical Properties' stock price down with it.

Investors (Unwisely) Dumped Everything Adeptus Touched

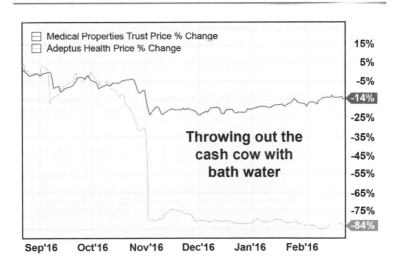

As with Omega, this was an Adeptus-specific problem rather than a Medical Properties issue. Ed's experienced management team was able to get Adeptus back in line and continued operating without a business hitch. (Worst case? They would have dumped Adeptus and taken a minor one-time hit to cash flow. That would have presented another buying opportunity, because it wouldn't have affected the business long term).

Interest rates are another headline worry that won't affect the company materially or over long periods of time. Medical Properties IPO'd in July 2005 when the Fed was boosting rates from 1% to 5.25%. Medical Properties did just fine. We have no reason to expect differently if rates continue to rise.

For second-level thinkers, pullbacks like these provide buying opportunities when stock prices "fall behind" the rising dividend trend.

The Dividend Yield Trendline: A Buy Signal

A simple way to judge a potential REIT bargain is to consider its current yield with respect to its historical range. If the current yield exceeds the historical norm, it may well be time to buy.

For example, let's map Omega Healthcare's trailing 12-month (TTM) dividend yield versus its stock price over the last 11 years. Notice that when its yield (darker line) is high, it's a pretty reliable indicator that its share price (lighter line) is low—and due to rally.

Buy the Peaks in Yield (Which Are Usually Price Bottoms)

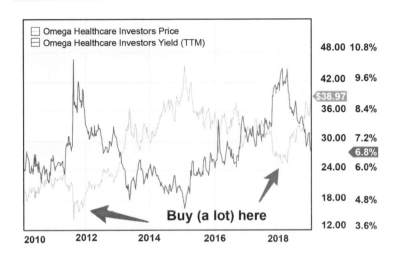

It's similar with Medical Properties. When its yield is high, its price is too low.

Again, Buy the Yield High (Because Price Is Low)

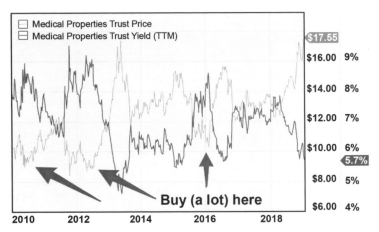

(Please note that the "price-only" lines in the two charts above dramatically understate total returns. They don't include dividends.)

It's easy to time your purchases with these types of charts alone. We aren't talking "market timing," though. We are talking smart times to buy based on valuation and dividend yield. Buy timeless REITs like these when their yields are high and hold for rising income and price gains over time.

Omega Heathcare's recent rally has lowered its yield to 6.8%. It's still a good buy today, but no longer a great one—the result of price appreciation! Remember, we outlined 10 REIT ideas in the beginning of this chapter. Each of these 10 stocks pays more than 7% and has raised its dividend by 15% or more over the last three years.

More No Withdrawal Stocks: Commercial Landlords

HIGH-YIELD ASSET CLASS	AVERAGE YIELD
Commercial Landlords	7.8%
Floating-Rate Bonds	6.7%
"Go Anywhere" Bond Funds	8.0%
Infrastructure Plays	6.4%
Recession-Proof REITs	7.5%
Secure, Boring Bonds	6.5%

Commercial loan firms are often structured as REITs. Their businesses are generally more complex than standard landlording, so a lender with a bit of subject matter expertise can really set itself apart from the pretenders. Also, the need for commercial financing is booming; such loans are up tenfold in the last eight years. Yet banks are leaving the business!

Banking is basically a game in which banks decide how much cash they should hold onto and how much to lend out. The best banks know their customers and have a pretty good idea what their risks are. But today, banks are remote from their customers and few lenders retain their loans. They serve shareholders, which makes sense, but their incentive is to lend out everything they have in search of higher profits (cash lying around isn't earning anything). Capital requirements set by regulators are often all that hold the least responsible back.

Anything deemed "high-risk speculation" is no longer

acceptable for banks. Most don't want to deal with the headaches, so they stepped away from the commercial market. Their flight provides opportunities for non-bank lenders such as Ladder Capital.

Ladder not only writes mortgages for commercial properties, but it also invests in highly rated (which is crucial) commercial mortgage-backed securities (CMBSs) and commercial real estate equity too. It's not a bank, so the firm is free to pursue different opportunities depending on market conditions.

Ladder's "interest rate resistance" is an attractive trait too. Thanks to the firm's $1.2 billion floating-rate portfolio and various interest rate hedges, management has estimated that a 100-basis point increase in LIBOR would boost annual net interest income by $3.3 million. That's right; Ladder does *better* when rates rise. Who's afraid of the Big Bad Fed now?

LADR Per Share Earnings Increase with in LIBOR

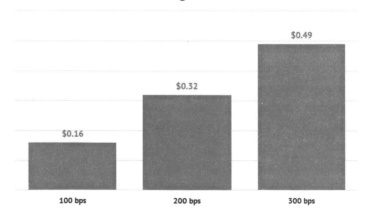

If rate hikes slow, is that bad for Ladder? Its loan portfolio is 72% floating rate, after all. But it does not *rely* on rising rates to increase net income. The company continues to ramp up its loan *volume*, which is the real driver of higher earnings (and higher dividends for us.)

We first recommended the stock in September 2016 for its safe 8.3% yield and dividend growth potential. Since then, Ladder has delivered the goods—*four dividend hikes plus two year-end special dividends.* We have collected $3.49 in dividends on an initial purchase of just $13.74. In other words, *we've recouped 25.4% of our initial investment already in cash.*

The large dividend with upside has attracted its share of attention from other income-focused investors. Ladder's charmed payout has helped the stock provide us with 58.5% total returns—nearly double the S&P 500 over the same timeframe! (Plus, our yield on cost is 9.9% and climbing.)

Ladder Pays More and Appreciates More Too

Arbor Realty Trust (ABR) is another commercial lender that's been humming. Over the last five years, Arbor has tended to pay between 7% and 9%. Yet it pays more today. This is simply a case of a stock price not being able to "keep up" with rapid dividend increases, even though the underlying business has never been better!

When Dividends Move "Too Fast" for Their Stocks

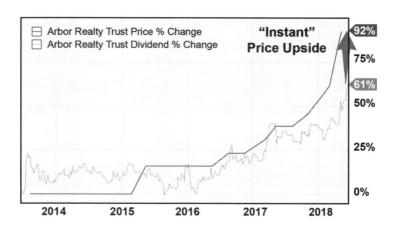

Arbor's price was lagging because its double-digit yield appeared "too good to be true." It wasn't for high-quality Arbor, but high yields can signal dumpster fires for others with weaker business models. Mortgage REITs come to mind because their 10%+ current yield can be a trap if you don't watch your step in this sector.

Be Careful with mREITs

Mortgage REITs (mREITs), like Ladder and Arbor,

don't own buildings. They own paper. Specifically, they buy mortgage loans and collect the interest. How do they make money? By borrowing short and lending long. That is, borrow money at lower rates and lend it out at higher rates.

This business model "prints" money when long-term rates are steady or, better yet, declining. When long-term rates drop, these existing mortgages become more valuable (because new loans pay less).

Everyone loves mREITs thanks to their fat yields. Check out these dividends!

TICKER	FIRM	YIELD
AGNC	AGNC Investment	12.0%
CIM	Chimera Investment	10.6%
MFA	MFA Financial	11.1%
NLY	Annaly Capital	11.6%
NRZ	New Residential Investment	12.2%
TWO	Two Harbors Investments	10.0%

As Tom's father was fond of warning, there is no such thing as a free lunch. The traditional mREIT's gravy train derails when rates rise and these mortgage portfolios *decline* in value. Historically, rising-rate environments have been very bad for mREITs and have resulted in deadly dividend cuts.

For example, investors in industry poster child Annaly Capital (NLY) took it on the chin during the last rate hike cycle. When Alan Greenspan boosted rates from June 2004 to June 2006, everyone knew higher rates would be problematic, but Annaly investors didn't run for the exits until *after* it chopped its payout in mid-2005.

mREIT Investors Were Blindsided in 2005

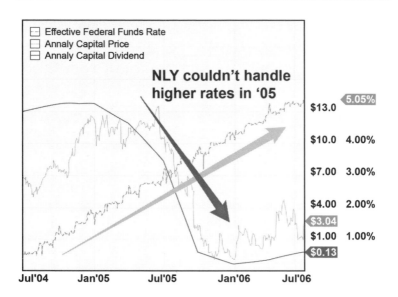

A double-digit yield is great, but it's not enough to withstand a dividend cut. Stocks can easily drop by 50% or more, just as Annaly did when its payouts got chopped, costing its investors years' worth of dividends overnight!

Now, give Annaly's management team credit—they adjusted and were better prepared for *this* rate hike cycle. The firm had hedged its portfolio and diversified into commercial loans. The result has been 47% total returns since the Fed began hiking in late 2015.

10+ Years Later, Annaly Was Better Prepared

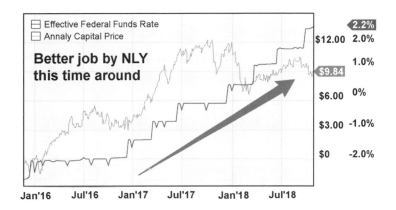

We can do better than Annaly though. New Residential Investment has doubled its investors' money and the value of its own portfolio (its book value) in less than three years. They knew something that other mREITs didn't!

NRZ's Smart Pivot Paid Off

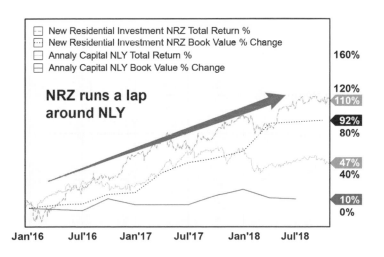

The firm's source of extra profits, as discussed earlier, was its investment in MSRs (mortgage service rights). They tend to rise in value when mortgage refinancing slows down, and "refi" activity has slowed significantly in recent years. As long as this environment continues, New Residential will be the mREIT to own. At the time of this writing, only 5% of outstanding mortgage loans in the US were refinanceable. This is good for the company, its dividend, and its stock price.

Only 5% of Loans Are Refinanceable (Good for New Residential)

Be Careful with BDCs Too

As they do with mREITs, most income investors find their way to business development companies (BDCs) by screening or searching for big yields. And there's no doubt these listed payouts do appear impressive! Here are the five largest BDCs (per assets under management).

TICKER	FIRM	YIELD
ARCC	Ares Capital	9.6%
AINV	Apollo Investment	12.0%
PSEC	Prospect Capital	10.6%
FSK	FS KKR Capital	12.0%
MAIN	Main Street Capital	6.4%

A first-level look at the table above might have you wondering why anyone would buy Main Street Capital when they could almost double their dividend by choosing another ticker. There is a good reason, but first let's talk about what BDCs actually *do* so that we can understand what is driving these big dividends.

It all started in 1940, when Congress passed the Investment Company Act. It created a new form of lending with tax benefits similar to those currently enjoyed by REITs. To put it simply, firms that lend to certain types of small companies get a pass on their tax bill if they pay out most (at least 90%) of their income to shareholders as dividends. Hence the big yields you see above.

Also, many of these loans have floating-rate kickers, so BDCs are positioned to make money in any rate environment. Really, they have a sweet setup. The problem is, their setup may be a little too sweet for the small niche they are all trying to serve. What's to stop a small company from shopping around for its capital, driving BDC earnings down because they have to offer lower rates to lower quality borrowers in order to profit?

Over the long haul, very few BDCs deliver their dividends without tapping their investors' pockets. That is, they fund their payouts partly from the income they derive from their loans (which is good) and partly by selling investors' assets (which, of course, is bad). Here's the tell—over the last five years, only Main Street has delivered total returns above its promised dividend.

Empty Payout Promises: 4 of 5 BDCs Underperform Their Yields

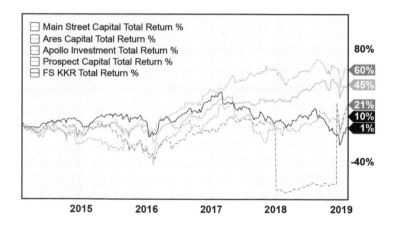

Two simple yet important things set Main Street apart:

1. The firm increases its investment income annually, and

2. It pays a conservative dividend so that it never has to cut it.

Since its IPO in 2007, Main Street has boosted its dividend (which is paid monthly) a lovely 77%. It's never been cut. The company smartly keeps a buffer and pays out extra income as a year-end special dividend to make sure its investors (who depend on its monthly dividend to pay the bills) are never short.

MAIN Dividends Per Share (Trailing 12 Months)

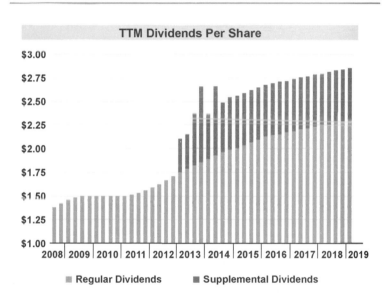

What's so hard about this? Apparently, a lot. Three of Main Street's four competitors are paying *lower* dividends today than they were five years ago. This shows that their lending businesses actually become *less and less* valuable over time. These stocks, always living on borrowed time, are *not* the types of investments we want in our No Withdrawal Portfolio.

Two Dividend Dogs

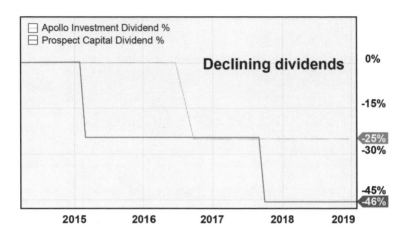

So should we buy Main Street Capital and call it a day? It's not that easy. As always, the price we pay matters. While most BDCs trade at a discount to their NAV, Main Street consistently trades at a premium. The trick with the company is to pay as little a premium as possible, because dips in the price-to-book ratio (below 1.3 or so) tend to indicate bargains in the stock price.

Dips in Price-to-Book Are Buying Opps for MAIN

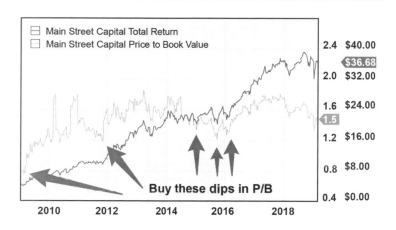

Main Street isn't quite there today, but it's a good income stock to keep on your watch list. Other BDCs, however, tend to be yield traps. Always check the long-term track record and, unless you see one that is shaping up like Main Street's, you should probably stay away.

Three Parting Words for REIT (and REIT-like) Investing

Watch out for debt

REITs are different from other stocks, where shrinking share counts are desirable. That's not how the REIT game of Monopoly is played. Here, management strives to acquire as many cash-producing assets as it can. And it funds these acquisitions by either borrowing money or by selling (offering) more of their own common stock.

You can see that since it was founded, Ladder consistently expanded its loan portfolio through the first of the two methods—borrowing:

Ladder's 51% Annual Loan Growth

Ladder's weighted average loan-to-value (LTV) ratio is a conservative 68%, which means they have a sizeable 32% equity cushion in case real estate prices decline again. The bank doesn't lose out until the market value of the collateral—what it could realize if it had to sell the collateral to satisfy its loan—drops below 32%. Contrast this with your average homebuyer who has, at most, a 20% equity cushion via the down payment. And in most cases, as we saw during the housing crisis, it's much less! Ladder's 68% means it has *A-1 credit quality.*

Look for internal management

No less important than the other criteria we have discussed for selecting great REITs is management. As with bond funds, you want to be backing great managers. Warren Buffett's sidekick, Charlie Munger, calls it backing the jockey, not the horse. A decent horse (business) with a great jockey (manager) can do much better than a good to great horse with a mediocre jockey.

A red flag from the get-go is this. Some REITs are often externally managed. This means that their assets are housed within the company itself, but the asset management decisions—what to buy and what to sell—are "outsourced" to a third-party management team in exchange for a fee. The fee is usually based on assets under management. The incentive is wrong. To make more money, the managers must grow assets, and while their value may increase, it's easy to borrow ill-advisedly to boost assets, but that debt eventually comes due.

While internal management is best almost exclusively, there are rare exceptions. Sometimes external management makes perfect sense and can even be a big advantage. For example, Blackstone Mortgage Trust benefits greatly from the expertise and hookups of its parent company and external manager, Blackstone (BX).

In 2013, Blackstone bet on the commercial real estate market. It spun off Blackstone Mortgage Trust and raised $660 million in initial capital to get the business off the ground. But this wasn't a typical spinoff, where the new company is left to find its own way in the business world. Here, Mortgage Trust remains under the loving care and management of Blackstone. While Mortgage Trust itself now has over $13 billion in assets and a market capitalization of $4 billion, it benefits from the expertise, clout, and war chest of its parent company. Each has an interest in the other's welfare.

Choosing Mortgage Trust here is the same as when we

contrarian income investors buy municipal bonds and look to the industry experts at Nuveen—because they have the inside track on the best muni deals. Likewise, we should aspire to buy commercial real estate through industry experts like Blackstone, which has its hooks everywhere. Blackstone is an active investor across the US and Europe. It commands over $100 billion of investor capital, deployed by hundreds of real estate professionals in offices around the world.

Recently, Blackstone Mortgage Trust was borrowing money for just LIBOR +2%. This dirt-cheap borrowing rate is a unique benefit of still being managed by Blackstone. This "almost free" money lets the firm chase down loans that are bigger than even the big banks can hold.

Another benefit of having access to (read: sharing) Blackstone's management team is the know-how and expertise to write a smart deal (for a 1% fee, of course). Again, its weighted average loan-to-value (LTV) ratio is a conservative 62%—which means they have a big 38% equity cushion against real estate price declines. This is a bigger cash buffer than Ladder's, which is saying something.

As a second-level thinker, you would have asked why 8% was available at the time of this IPO. That high a yield can often signal trouble. Yet there were two reasons why Mortgage Trust was so cheap and therefore its yield so high, and neither was a problem for those willing to look further. First, the "spinoff" itself was still relatively new, and new companies are perceived as riskier—even if they have the backing of a parent like Blackstone.

Second, Mortgage Trust is grouped with mREITs at large,

and investors view those as complicated and risky. Yet while the company is technically a writer of mortgages that is also structured as a REIT, it has no genetic similarities to Annaly. It has a beautifully simple business model, a stellar pedigree, and a $100+ billion war chest backing it—the benefits of a strong parent. (The stock *still* yields a generous 7.4%. We believe the firm will begin raising its dividend in the near future, and when it does, that will likely provide its stock price with a nice catalyst.)

But Mortgage Trust is the rare exception to the "no externally managed REITs" rule. Externally managed REITs typically underperform their counterparts that have the "luxury" of in-house management teams. Almost exclusively you want to seek out those REITs that are internally managed.

You want inside ownership

Let's look again at Ladder. During 2018, Ladder received a buyout offer of $15 per share. This is where having management's interests well aligned with investors' really matters.

The firm's primary asset is the expertise of its senior management team, which averages 28 years of industry experience. In 2018, management purchased nearly five times as many shares as they sold. Insiders own $239 million of equity—12% of the firm's market cap. That's excellent and very unusual for a REIT.

Thanks to their significant skin in the game, Ladder management came through for investors and rejected the lowball offer. *Shares are up more than 30% since management rejected the bid.* Investors benefited from management's long-term view.

Generally, you don't see much inside share ownership in REITs and related equities, so it's a good indicator of "excellence" when there is.

CHAPTER 9

Building Your Portfolio

IT'S ONE THING to pick remarkable REITs and brilliant bond CEFs. It's another to organize them in a way that maximizes long-term income and capital gains growth and minimizes risk. Importantly, how many stocks and funds should you buy?

We recommend a portfolio of 15 to 20 positions, about 50% in stocks and 50% in bond CEFs. Owning this many holdings reduces the negative effect of one blowing up—which can happen to even the most careful investor. On the other hand, this is concentrated enough so that good things can be … good! You don't want to be a mutual fund, which dilutes the benefits of this strategy, and you don't want to be so concentrated you have to worry about one bad stock ruining your whole retirement. After all, you are supposed to be retired, when whatever you are doing is fun, rewarding in non-monetary ways, and so on.

No rebalancing

Once you have picked your starting portfolio, you don't have to do much. We definitely are not fans of "rebalancing," where you reduce your winners and buy more of your losers monthly, quarterly, or annually. We'd rather buy what we'd like to own for a long time and only sell when the business fundamentals no longer promise growing income or when another security goes on clearance sale, for example. Ideally, we'd never sell, but management and businesses change.

Remember, the 8% No Withdrawal Portfolio is not about whether your portfolio is up or down: it's about whether your income keeps growing.

Otherwise, market hiccups, drops, or even crashes don't matter. Remember, the 8% No Withdrawal Portfolio is *not* about whether your portfolio is up or down: *it's about whether your income keeps growing.* Let's look at a reasonable scenario. Start with 7% for the annual dividend yield alone and assume that it rises 2% a year across the entire portfolio. That is, the bond yields are flat and the REIT yields increase about 4% a year.

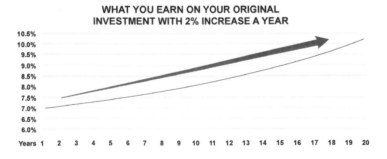

WHAT YOU EARN ON YOUR ORIGINAL
INVESTMENT WITH 2% INCREASE A YEAR

In year 20, you are reaping a whopping 10.2% on your original investment. This is without any allowance for the REIT stock prices increasing with yield. This is *only* growth in the percentage paid out on your initial investment. You know how cost of living adjustments—COLAs—have all but disappeared? You can estimate a 2% annual "COLA" in your 8% No Withdrawal Portfolio while you don't touch your principal.

Now, this is where the REIT part of the portfolio comes in handy. We can't assume low 2% inflation a year forever, and you will still see increases in things like food and energy, perhaps, even if you have paid off your home and don't rent. REIT rental contracts typically include inflation escalators. They will vary according to type of real estate, but they are added protection. This won't increase your real return—"real" meaning your return minus inflation—but it will help safeguard it. And over 20 years, that's really important. Which brings us to another important point besides "inflation safety," which is "safety of principal."

The typical financial planner or advisor works with what's called a "glide path." (It's also what so-called retirement "target date" funds use, more or less, differing by choice of investments and when rebalancing is performed.) In ye olden days, we were advised to put our age in bonds (fixed income) and the rest in equities (stocks of operating businesses). If you were 60, then you'd have 60% of your investment accounts invested in bonds and 40% in stocks. By 90, it would be 90% bonds and 10% stocks. You'd "glide," making small adjustments every year along the way.

It may seem like a smart move, but going lean on stocks

leaves you open to two big risks:

- That inflation will eat away your savings, and

- You'll miss out on the long-term gains only the stock market can offer to help you survive inflation.

Consider these numbers from the Society of Actuaries: If you're a 65-year-old man, you have a 41% chance of living to 85 and 20% odds of hitting 90. If you're a woman of the same age, your chances jump to 53% that you'll make 85 and 32% for 90.

And here's the part most retirees overlook: if you're married, the odds one of you will still be around at 85 takes a big leap to 72%. Marriage is good for our health, as is being a woman!

Longer lifespans are good news, provided your portfolio is also built for the long run. This means you need healthy servings of stocks to protect you from the ills of inflation. But we don't want to water down our income stream either, because that can mean selling investments and withdrawing that capital detrimentally. We must avoid the reverse dollar-cost averaging trap at all cost.

This is where the 8% No Withdrawal Portfolio works even more magic. The new thinking says the biggest risk to retirement savings is in, say, the five to 10 years *before* you retire. That's when taking a huge market hit can readjust all your estimates. If you plan to have $1 million, for instance, in the 8% No Withdrawal strategy, your gross income would be $80,000. But let's say it's 2007, and you are planning on that in a few months or a year. During the 2000–2002 and 2008–

2009 crashes, a few people I know had to put off retirement plans for a number of years to save up more money.

We can't know when a crash is coming. People who try to time a crash go to cash too early or, even if their timing is good, they "get back in" too late. No one can time the market and "go to cash" or "get back in" at the right times. It's like the broken clock that's right twice a day. There's all the rest of the time.

Market crashes come typically without warning and are very fast. So, the new thinking says that because the biggest risk is *before* you retire, up your bonds to 80%—you read right—and then shift back *after* you retire, so that by age 90, you are actually 90% in stocks and 10% in bonds. And that's not crazy, either, because the longer you will live, the more inflation risk you face.

We are not retirement academic researchers, but we think 80% in fixed income that long before retirement isn't feasible for most people. Rather, we recommend that in the years before retirement—five to 10, say—you start the 8% No Withdrawal Portfolio strategy. Instead of taking out the income as you will later, reinvest all dividends. Your discount online broker can do this automatically by, in most cases, checking a box. Then, when you retire, uncheck the box and collect the income.

We can't say this enough. This book isn't about estimating your income, capital gains,

> **Start the 8% No Withdrawal strategy at least five to 10 years before retirement.**

and withdrawals to die with zero dollars—though for anyone who doesn't care about leaving money to anyone or anything, it's a laudable goal! Remember, you are only concerned with the income. You aren't withdrawing your principal. And this simple strategy is a way to grow your income even though you aren't working. Hard to beat.

This is a solid King Solomon approach. It "splits the baby" of bonds and stocks, builds in rising income, and offers inflation help through the REITs. You don't have to sit down every January and adjust your portfolio. You do need to keep up somewhat with how the REIT businesses are doing, but you would have to do that with any stocks you owned anyway. And as you age, you can decide to draw on your principal if you want, because you will have plenty of it. And if you don't need all the income, simply reinvest it!

When should you sell a stock or fund?

Don't be afraid to sell if the story, facts, or fundamentals change from your initial purchase. And don't worry about your initial purchase price if and when this happens—just sell and move on.

For example, Brett advised subscribers to sell Brookfield Real Assets Income Fund (RA) in late 2018, even though the fund yielded 10%. We hadn't made any money on the investment because the fund was increasingly tapping its own NAV to pay its dividend (its interest payments weren't enough to fund its distribution, even with its use of cheap money leverage). Brookfield Real Assets' NAV *declined.*

A Declining NAV Indicated Trouble for Brookfield Real Assets

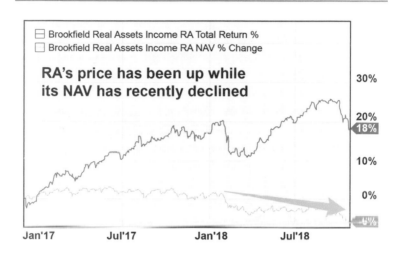

☐ Brookfield Real Assets Income RA Total Return %
☐ Brookfield Real Assets Income RA NAV % Change

RA's price has been up while its NAV has recently declined

Brett had earlier recommended selling one of our favorite 9% payers, the Aberdeen Asia-Pacific Income Fund, for a similar reason. The bond market's backdrop had changed, and the fund's holdings, while high quality, were largely fixed rate in nature. A rising interest rate environment in the US was putting pressure on its bond prices, and its bonds didn't pay enough to cover its 9% distribution from income alone. So Brett issued a controversial sell rating on the fund to book profits. We're glad we sold because the fund's price headed lower after we walked it to the exit.

Knowing When to Sell Is Important

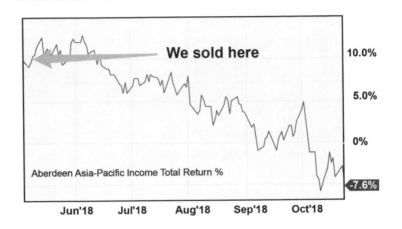

Aberdeen Asia-Pacific Income Total Return %

We sold here

10.0%

5.0%

0%

-7.6%

Jun'18   Jul'18   Aug'18   Sep'18   Oct'18

Should you use a "trailing stop" to tell you when to sell?

If you're not familiar with the concept of a stop-loss, or a trailing stop, it's simply the point at which you define when you're going to sell. For example, you might decide that you're going to sell a stock if it drops 20% below your buy price (a 20% stop) or if it fades 20% off a recent high (a 20% trailing stop).

In theory, it's foolproof. Stops help you limit your losses while letting your winners run. In practice, though, *you'll often end up selling at the worst possible time.*

Say you had a 20% trailing stop in place. You could end up selling a great stock based on first-level thinkers driving a stock down for the wrong reasons.

Take Omega, for example. Its stock price implies dividend drama that doesn't appear to be real. A stop-loss would instruct you to sell at times like this, when the *price is low* and *yield is high*.

Why "Stop Out" When Yield Is High (& Price Is Low)?

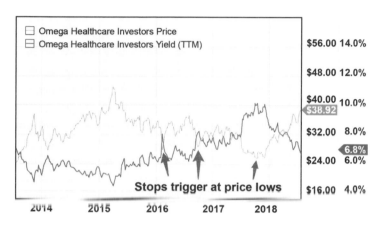

□ Omega Healthcare Investors Price
⊟ Omega Healthcare Investors Yield (TTM)

$56.00 14.0%

$48.00 12.0%

$40.00 10.0%
$38.92

$32.00 8.0%

6.8%
$24.00 6.0%

Stops trigger at price lows $16.00 4.0%

2014 2015 2016 2017 2018

While stops can certainly help *traders* hoping to catch the meat of a trend, they bury many dividend *investors*. The argument for stop-losses is based on the "wisdom" of prices. If the market knows something we don't, then it's best for us to respect that knowledge. The problem is that the market can be pretty dumb when it comes to dividend analysis!

We're better off asking ourselves: "Is the dividend safe?" If we believe it is, we should take advantage of any pullback *to buy more* when prices are low and yields are high.

One more thing. *Stop-loss orders often don't work.* If emotional selling hits a stock, many sell orders don't get executed as the price plummets. They fail just when you need them.

We suggest leaving the stops for the trend followers and buy-and-hope types. Focus instead on buying bargains. There's no guaranteed way to time your sales. Each stock is its own separate case. We recommend constructing and sticking with portfolios that deliver safe 8%+ yields over time (with long-term price stability) thanks to our two core principles:

1. We buy stocks and funds when they are out of favor, so that prices are lower and yields are higher when we purchase.

2. We rely on dividends alone for income, so that price ups and downs do not affect us.

Thanks to an 11-year-old bull market, stocks *in general* are expensive. But as long as there are headlines, there will be headline worries. And thanks to them, whether real news or fake, we're able to find pockets of value—cheap stocks, *in specific*. Even today.

Should you sell ("write") covered calls on your No Withdrawal Portfolio?

A manic stock market is perfect for covered call writers. When volatility is high, so are option premiums, which means this popular income strategy should be a particularly profitable one as long as the market is rocky.

New to covered calls? Here's how they work.

1. You buy at least 100 shares of a stock or fund. You now own these outright. (Why 100? Because one

covered call contract covers 100 shares of underlying stock.)

2. You then sell ("write") covered calls at a price around or above the stock's current price for additional income. In doing so, you are agreeing to sell the stock at that price—the "strike"—in exchange for money *today*.

Covered calls can be an effective way to increase the cash flow from the stocks you already own. Since we're focused on cash, we prefer (as usual) to start with dividend-paying investments. Calls are a way to "accelerate" a stock's payout.

Here are a couple of real-life examples. A savvy reader asked us about selling covered calls on the DoubleLine Income Solutions Fund, the vehicle run by the "bond god" Jeffrey Gundlach himself. The fund yields an impressive 9.7% today with plenty of cash flow to cover the dividend. Its top five holdings pay plenty, boasting coupons of 9.25%, 8.25%, 8.43%, 12.32%, and 8.25%, respectively!

This makes covered calls a smart strategy, but also one that's limited by the fund's option availabilities. For example, we have to look out many months to get any reasonable premium on DoubleLine's Income Solutions calls. Here are the current quotes:

A Long Time Out and Not Much Premium

DSL Aug 16		210 Days to Expiration	
Calls	Bid	Ask	Last
$20 Call	$0.15	$0.30	$0.20

This means we can receive an extra $0.20 per share today if we sell calls that "strike" at $20 for DoubleLine. In other words, if the fund pops above $20 between now and August 16, we have to sell it for "just" $20 (and not $21 or $22 or whatever).

Shares trade for just $18.62 today, so this might be a tradeoff we're willing to make for an "instant" 1.1% bonus payout. (When we sell calls, we receive the premiums as cash in our account immediately. And remember, it's one call contract per 100 shares we own.)

But since our call doesn't expire for another 210 days, we can't quite run it twice a year. So we're only looking at an extra 2% yield annually. While that's better than nothing, and 11.7% annually is nothing to sneeze at, we can do better.

We should consider high-yield *stocks*—not CEFs— with more trading volume. This usually means that we have more call options to choose from and more income to collect. Let's consider Omega Healthcare Investors, which yields 6.8% today and has its dividend well covered by the rents of its tenants (who operate skilled nursing facilities).

Omega does not pay what DoubleLine does, but it offers more options, more often. Here's what we mean.

Shares trade for about $38.06 as we write. There are March calls that "strike" at $39 (which means we are sellers *at* $39 per share if Omega trades above that price on March 15). They are fetching $0.53 per share, offering an "instant" 1.4% payout.

Less Time Out with More Premium Too

OHI Mar 15		56 Days to Expiration	
Calls	Bid	Ask	Last
$39 Call	$0.50	$0.60	$0.53

But here's the key. When these calls "expire" 56 days from now, we can write *another* set of covered calls for *more* income. In fact, there are two ways this trade can work out for us:

1. If Omega closes above $39.00 per share on March 15, then we'll keep our $0.53 in call premiums (or $53 per contract because they come in lots of 100 shares). We'll also sell our shares at $39, which means we'll pocket an additional $0.94 per share (or $94 per contract) in capital gains.

2. If Omega closes below $39 that day, we'll still own our shares. We'll still have made our $53 in cash per contract from this trade. And we can then write a new set of calls.

Worst case, we'll accelerate Omega's dividend from 6.8% to 15.9% *yearly* if we continue to sell calls on our shares. Best case, we'll keep the call income *and* the capital gains *and* the first quarter's dividend, for a neat 32% annualized return!

PARTING WORDS

We know that this book disagrees with most retirement planning out there, and don't get us wrong—we're glad that there are "target date" funds for people and that no-load low-cost fund companies like Vanguard offer them. All in all, anything that helps people make sensible decisions with their lifetime of savings is a good thing.

But our goal here is to show that for those of you planning to live off your investments in whole or in part, you can have more income, live better than you thought, and maintain your principal. You won't see it at the big shops like Merrill Lynch, Wells Fargo, Morgan Stanley, or JPMorgan Chase, not because they don't know what you've just read, but because they are dealing with too much client money. They can only invest their clients in pretty much the same things everyone else is buying—the biggest, most liquid securities. For them to invest only a fraction of their clients in the 8% No Withdrawal Retirement Portfolio would use up all the shares traded in our CEFs and REITs for months and months—and likely years and years. And even then, their buying would drive the prices up too much! They just can't do it. *You can.*

If you would like to explore this strategy further, we'd love to chat with you. You can always subscribe to the *Contrarian Income Report*, become a client of Tom's, or do a bit of both. This doesn't have to be your only strategy, either. But for your retirement income investments, it's easy to see the advantages of putting some money to work in the 8% No Withdrawal Retirement Portfolio.

Appendix A: Frequently Asked Questions (FAQs)

What is dollar-cost averaging (DCA)?

You commit to investing money in the same stocks and/ or funds on a regular basis. In doing so, you'll naturally buy more shares when prices are low and fewer when prices are high. This evens out your buy price, so you aren't buying at highs or lows.

For example, let's say you invest new money today into your portfolio. Then, the market plunges 10% in the next month and takes your account with it. This pullback will actually be good news for you, because your next contribution will fetch more shares, and more shares mean more dividends! With DCA, you benefit from lower prices and you are more cautious as prices rise. You won't get whipsawed by short term movements in your stock or the market, and you don't have guess whether "the market is high" or "the market is low." After all, studies have demonstrated that even if the very rare investor somehow manages to "get out" and go to cash at the right time, that investor doesn't reinvest at the "right time." (Tom has a friend who cashed out in the fall of 2007 (great!), but has never returned to the market, missing out on a decade of terrific returns (not great). This is the rule rather than the exception for those who try to time.) That means selling low and buying high, which guarantees losing money—even if over time the market rises.

Bottom line? DCA is a way to sleep at night.

Dollar-cost averaging helped build your retirement portfolio. You bought stock regularly over many years, mostly through contributions to your company's 401(k) plan or other retirement savings method. Doing so smoothed out your purchase prices, so you didn't get caught investing only at high times and you kept investing at low times. (It's also why this book's method is important, because without it you "reverse DCA" when withdrawing in retirement, selling low.)

DCA works, but there is one important requirement. You have to be firm and not waver—not be emotional—no matter what the market does. And that's exactly the point of using it.

Wait. Isn't this portfolio designed to never go down?

Our strategy is designed so that you never have to sell shares into a downturn. You'll never have to employ "reverse dollar-cost averaging" because we're only concerned with dividends, which are much less manic than the broader stock market.

This is an important distinction. We have a No Withdrawal Portfolio, *not* a "Never Go Down" portfolio. A Never Go Down Portfolio would consist of cash and US Treasuries and wouldn't pay you enough income to retire on. You'd have to withdraw money and risk running out of cash in your retirement!

How do I stay ahead of inflation?

Make sure your portfolio's total dividends are growing faster than the current rate of inflation. For example, let's say inflation is running at about 2% (a reasonable assumption today). We'll want to see our portfolio's dividends growing by 2% or better to stay ahead of inflation.

Some payments will be static, while others will be growing by 5% or better annually. Variation is fine. But when we blend everything together, we do want to see our total dividends growing faster than inflation.

How does the 8% No Withdrawal Portfolio work in a traditional IRA or Inherited IRA where there is a Required Minimum Distribution (RMD)?

Very well, but not indefinitely. Unlike a taxable account, a traditional (or rollover) IRA account owner must take an annual required minimum distribution (RMD). The amount depends on the IRS's table for your age. Here is the latest IRS worksheet for calculating the RMD:

IRA Required Minimum Distribution Worksheet

Use this worksheet to figure this year's required withdrawal for your traditional IRA UNLESS your spouse[1] is the sole beneficiary of your IRA and he or she is more than 10 years younger than you.

Deadline for receiving required minimum distribution:
- Year you turn age 70 ½ - by April 1 of the following year
- All subsequent years - by December 31 of that year

1. IRA balance[2] on December 31 of the previous year. $_____

2. Distribution period from the table below for your age on your birthday this year.   _____

3. Line 1 divided by number entered on line 2. This is your required minimum distribution for this year from this IRA. $_____

4. Repeat steps 1 through 3 for each of your IRAs.

Table III (Uniform Lifetime)

Age	Distribution Period	Age	Distribution Period	Age	Distribution Period	Age	Distribution Period
70	27.4	82	17.1	94	9.1	106	4.2
71	26.5	83	16.3	95	8.6	107	3.9
72	25.6	84	15.5	96	8.1	108	3.7
73	24.7	85	14.8	97	7.6	109	3.4
74	23.8	86	14.1	98	7.1	110	3.1
75	22.9	87	13.4	99	6.7	111	2.9
76	22.0	88	12.7	100	6.3	112	2.6
77	21.2	89	12.0	101	5.9	113	2.4
78	20.3	90	11.4	102	5.5	114	2.1
79	19.5	91	10.8	103	5.2	115 and over	1.9
80	18.7	92	10.2	104	4.9		
81	17.9	93	9.6	105	4.5		

Once you determine a separate required minimum distribution from each of your traditional IRAs, you can total these minimum amounts and take them from any one or more of your traditional IRAs.

For additional information, see:

- Publication 590-B, *Distributions from Individual Retirement Arrangements (IRAs)*
- Retirement Topics – Required Minimum Distributions

[1] Generally, your marital status is determined as of January 1 of each year. If your spouse is the beneficiary of your IRA on January 1, he or she remains a beneficiary only for purposes of calculating the required minimum distribution for that IRA even if you get divorced or your spouse dies during the year.

[2] You must increase your IRA balance by any outstanding rollover and recharacterized Roth IRA conversions that were not in any traditional IRA on December 31 of the previous year.

The Distribution Period decreases, increasing the amount of the RMD. Eventually, the RMD exceeds the annual No Withdrawal income in the account and you must take out principal. The exact age of this "crossover" is impossible to pinpoint because returns will vary, but in many scenarios, the point at which the RMD exceeds the annual account income is in the mid-to-late 80s. In these cases the account retains significant value well into the holder's late 90s and even beyond.

The table used for an Inherited IRA is different. The crossover in many scenarios occurs in the account owner's late 70s, which is somewhat earlier than for the traditional or rollover IRA, but the account retains significant value at about the same rate. And the person who inherited the IRA is accumulating other retirement assets too.

Appendix B: Tax Strategies for Popular Dividend Investments

While each investor's tax situation is different, and we do *not* provide personalized tax advice, we *have* put together a general overview of the tax status of the dividends in our portfolio.

Let's start with the most tax-efficient investments, which, thanks to their favored status, many investors hold in regular taxed accounts.

Municipal Bonds: Often Federal Tax-Exempt

Municipal, or "muni," bonds are issued by states, cities, and counties to raise money, usually for capital projects like public transportation and infrastructure improvements. Folks in high tax brackets love them because the interest paid by munis is often tax-exempt at the federal and/or state level.

That's right. The distributions you receive from funds such as the Nuveen Enhanced AMT-Free Municipal Credit Opportunities Fund are exempt from federal taxes. This means that their listed nominal yield is actually much higher because of the tax advantage. Nuveen provides a handy tool that lets you calculate the advantage—your "taxable equivalent yield"—on the fund's website.

When a 5.5% Yield Equals 9.3%

Taxable Equivalent Yield

Tax-Exempt Yield for Muni Fund NVG	5.5%
Filing Status	Joint ⌄
Federal Tax Rate	40.8% ⌄
Effective Tax Rate	40.8%
Calculate	9.3%

What looks like an okay-but-not-good-enough-for-us 5.5% becomes a juicy 9.3%.

Qualified Dividends: Maximum 20% Tax Rate

Investors receive "qualified dividends" from the common shares they own in regular US equities. Qualified dividends are taxed below the ordinary income rate. Their very favorable lower rate ranges from 0% to 20%, depending on your tax bracket.

Nonqualified Dividends: Taxed as Ordinary Income

In most cases, REIT (real estate investment trust) distributions, such as those dished out by Blackstone Mortgage Trust, are considered *nonqualified* dividends by the IRS. This means they are taxed at your regular income tax rate.

However, REIT investors now benefit from the tax breaks that "pass through" businesses receive. As a general rule, investors are allowed to deduct 20% of their REIT dividend income.

Interestingly, REIT income will be taxed at a lower rate than regular rental income, which would not receive the deduction—which means if you don't have a burning desire to change light bulbs and play landlord yourself, it will be cost effective to simply buy REITs, sit back, and let others hassle with physical properties!

Closed-End Funds: A Mix of Tax Categories

Each closed-end fund (CEF) has one or more categories of income that are passed onto you, the investor. Your tax rate depends on the blend of these four potential sources:

- Interest payments

- Dividends

- Capital gains

- Return of capital

For the specifics on how your funds' distributions were classified in previous years, you should contact them directly. This information typically appears on funds' web-sites. Also, Morningstar.com does provide a breakdown of the fund's latest distributions by income, short-term capital gains, long-term capital gains, and return of capital. For example, here's the breakdown for the BlackRock Floating Rate Income Strategies Fund (FRA).

Latest Distribution History FRA

	Income ?	S/T Cap Gain ?	L/T Cap Gain ?	Return Cap ?	Total
Year to Date (Est.)	0.4985	0.0000	0.0000	0.0000	0.4985
2017	0.7320	0.0000	0.0000	0.0000	0.7320
2016	0.9570	0.0000	0.0000	0.0000	0.9570
2015	0.7991	0.0000	0.0000	0.0705	0.8696
2014	0.7732	0.0000	0.0000	0.0685	0.8417

Annual distribution calculation is based on fund calendar year. Currency:USD

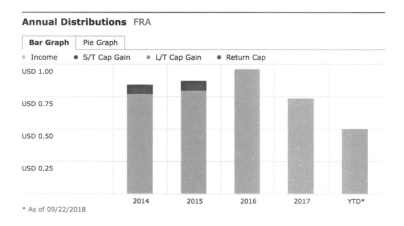

Annual Distributions FRA

| Bar Graph | Pie Graph |

• Income   • S/T Cap Gain   • L/T Cap Gain   • Return Cap

* As of 09/22/2018

Remember, management's primary goal is to make sure its distribution is fully funded. As a result, it usually doesn't provide investors with a "forecast" of how it plans to fund upcoming distributions, so that it has all options available at its disposal. But a quick review of previous distributions will give you a rough estimate of the current tax breakdown.

Avoiding the MLP "K-1 Headache"

Master limited partnerships (MLPs) are required to issue you a K-1 package at the end of the tax year. These are generally headaches for the person who does your taxes, whether it's you or a professional.

A few years ago, Brett's accountant calmly but sternly asked him to stop buying MLPs in his personal portfolio. He agreed and will pass the favor on to you. There are better places to find high yield anyway, which is why we do not own any MLPs in our income-generating portfolios. For example, there are MLP-focused CEFs that you can buy at a discount to NAV at certain times and avoid the K-1 headache (because they tend to issue 1099s instead, which are simpler to handle.)

Appendix C:
Additional Resources

As you build your own 8% No Withdrawal Portfolio, here are some online resources that you may find helpful.

Our ContrarianOutlook.com website publishes daily dividend-focused coverage and ideas. Sign up for our free daily newsletter and we'll send you a few great income investments every day.

The **Contrarian Income Report** is a premium service written, researched, and managed by Brett. For $99 per year, he will hold your hand and help you build your own portfolio with specific buy, hold, and sell recommendations. You can sign up for a risk-free free trial here: www.contrarianoutlook.com.

For a completely "hands off" No Withdrawal Portfolio, consider using Tom and Huckleberry Capital Management as your investment advisor. He'll manage your money for you (all kinds of accounts, $100,000 minimum investment). Learn more about Huckleberry's "Harvest" income and yield portfolio at www.investhuckleberry.com. You can reach Tom at tom@investhuckleberry.com and tom@tomjacobs.net

CEF Connect is the best screener for closed-end funds anywhere online. We use it ourselves. It is a great source of new ideas, and we have found the data (managed by Nuveen) to be accurate and insightful.

www.cefconnect.com

Finally, we both pay for our own subscriptions to YCharts. Along with CEF Connect, we used this platform to run the dividend-payer streams you read in this book. YCharts' "total return" calculation is also helpful in considering past dividend payments and their contributions to overall returns. (Many mainstream financial websites do not calculate this properly—YCharts does.)

www.ycharts.com

ABOUT THE AUTHORS

Brett Owens

EVER SINCE MY days at Cornell University and all through my years as a startup founder in Silicon Valley, I've hunted down safe, stable, meaningful yields.

For the last 10 years, I've been investing my startup profits and finding 6%, 7%, even 8%+ dividends with plenty of double digit gains along the way. In recent years, I started writing about the methods I use to generate these high levels of income.

Today I serve as chief investment strategist for the *Contrarian Income Report*—a publication that uncovers secure, high-yielding investments for thousands of investors. Since inception, my subscribers have generated total annualized returns of 11.4%, with the majority of these profits being delivered as monthly and quarterly dividends. In other words, they've collected safe 7% and 8% yields while they've kept their retirement capital intact. You may reach me at ContrarianOutlook.com.

Tom Jacobs

My parents were raised in the Great Depression and encouraged me to learn about money and business at a young age. Thanks to them, I bought my first stock with my Dad at age 12 and learned about compounding and dividend reinvestment. After attending Cornell University and the University of Chicago Law School, I kept investing through careers as a teacher and lawyer, and then The Motley Fool gave me the opportunity to invest full time.

Today, as a partner with Huckleberry Capital Management, I employ what I learned from my parents and the thinking in this book to help clients. Huckleberry manages over 100 individual accounts for clients in 25 states and three foreign countries from offices in Silicon Valley, Asheville, NC, and Marfa, TX. Please feel free to contact me at tom@investhuckleberry.com or tom@tomjacobs.net.

INDEX